The content contained within this book may not be reproduced, duplicated or transmitted without direct written permission from the author or the publisher.

Under no circumstances will any blame or legal responsibility be held against the publisher, or author, for any damages, reparation, or monetary loss due to the information contained within this book. Either directly or indirectly. You are responsible for your own choices, actions, and results.

Legal Notice:

This book is copyright protected. This book is only for personal use. You cannot amend, distribute, sell, use, quote or paraphrase any part, or the content within this book, without the consent of the author or publisher.

Disclaimer Notice:

Please note the information contained within this document is for educational and entertainment purposes only. All effort has been executed to present accurate, up to date, and reliable, complete information. No warranties of any kind are declared or implied. Readers acknowledge that the author is not engaging in the rendering of legal, financial, medical or professional advice. The content within this book has been derived from various sources. Please consult a licensed professional before attempting any techniques outlined in this book.

By reading this document, the reader agrees that under no circumstances is the author responsible for any losses, direct or indirect, which are incurred as a result of the use of the information contained within this document, including, but not limited to — errors, omissions, or inaccuracies.

TABLE

Of Contents

Round 1

Food

Hello, welcome to the Kids Against Parents Trivia Game.

Kids do you think that you are smarter than your parents? Parents do you still have it?

Well, it's time to find out who has the better brains.

So here is how the game works....

There are 2 teams. Team 1 will be the kids and team 2 will be the parents.

There are 20 rounds of questions and the objective is win more rounds than the other team.

The first half of each round will be the kids answering questions that the parents ask, and the second half will be the parents answering questions that the kids ask.

At the end of the round whatever team answers more questions right wins!

Pay attention to the instructions at the begging of each round because every few rounds there will be a special version of trivia with differing rules.

Scan below to see a 30 second video explaining the game.

Before we start round 1, let's do a practice question for each team.

Team Kids, you're up now (parents read the question)

Kids

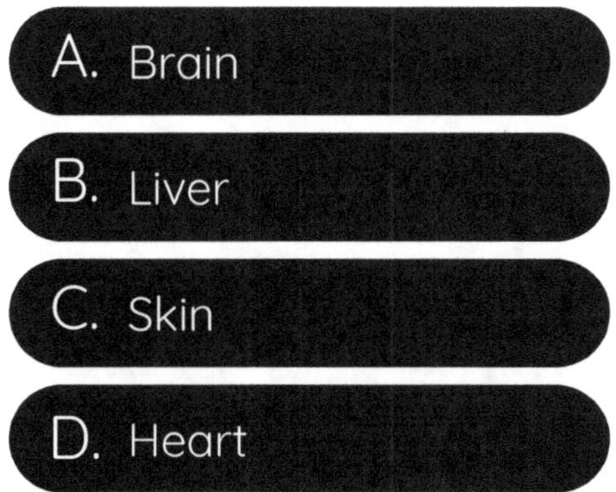

Answer: The heaviest organ is the

Yes, the skin is an organ, and on the average person, it makes up about 6% of your body weight. While the second largest organ, the liver is only about 2% of your body weight.

Team Parents, you're up now (kids ask the question)

Parents

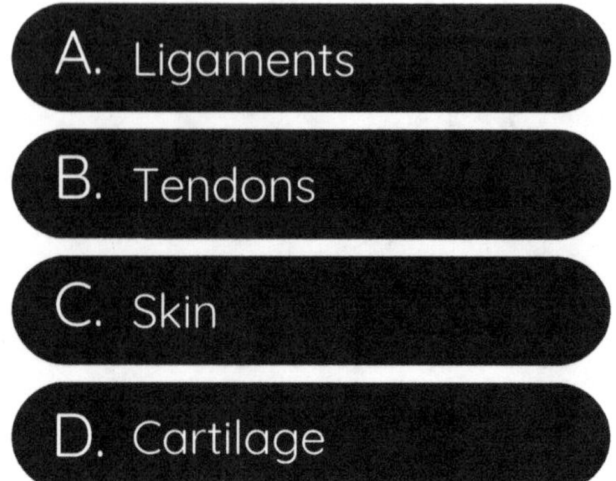

Answer: It is the

B. Tendons

Tendons are very strong and stretchy, which allows them to attach the muscle to the bones.

Get how the game works?

Now that you understand how the game works, let's get into round 1.

The category for this round is food.

This round has 9 questions.
Questions 1-7 are worth 1 point, while questions 8-9 will be worth 2 points

Good luck!

Kids

Parents

Keep score on this page by checking the boxes when a team answers the question correctly.

① ② ③ ④ ⑤ ⑥ ⑦ ⑧ ⑨

×2 Points

×2 Points

Total Points = __________

Total Points = __________

7

ROUND 1.1
QUESTIONS FOR KIDS

1 What is the main ingredient in Jell-O that gives it its form?

A. Disodium Phosphate

B. Gelatin

C. Sugar

D. Clear gel

Answer: The ingredient is

B. Gelatin

2 Which U.S. state is the biggest producer of coffee?

A. Florida

B. Idaho

C. California

D. Hawaii

Answer: The biggest producer of coffee in the U.S. is

D. Hawaii

3 What country first brought the mac and cheese recipe to America?

A. Germany

B. England

C. Columbia

D. France

Answer: The country is

D. France

Many think that Thomas Jefferson was responsible for bringing mac and cheese to America. During his time in France he loved mac and cheese so much that when he came back to the States, he hired a chef from France to come overseas and make mac and cheese for him.

4 I am a beer, yet kids can drink me and not get drunk. What am I?

Answer: I am Root Beer.

ROUND 1.1
QUESTIONS FOR KIDS

⑤ I have an ear but can not hear. What food am I?

Answer: I am corn.

⑥ Which U.S. city is known for having deep-dish pizza?

Answer: The city known for deep-dish pizza is Chicago.

⑦ Which country was the first chocolate bar created in?

Answer: It was created in England.

Before the chocolate bar was created in 1847, people primarily drank chocolate and added it to their milk and water.

⑧ What item of food gets stolen the most?

The most stolen food is cheese. About 4% of all cheese ends up stolen.

⑨ What food never expires?

Answer: Honey never expires.

Due to bees' unique enzymes, they are able to prevent bacteria from growing.

Random Fun Fact?

1 hamburger can have meat from up to 100 different cows.

ROUND 1.2
QUESTIONS FOR PARENTS

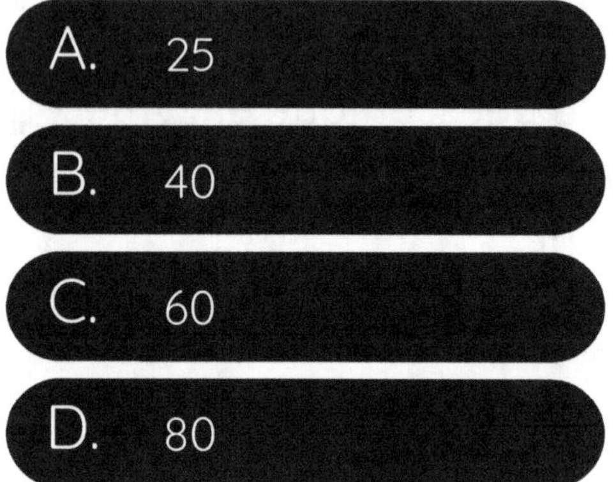

1 How many burgers does the average American eat every year?

A. 25

B. 40

C. 60

D. 80

Answer: The average American eats

C. 60 burgers per year

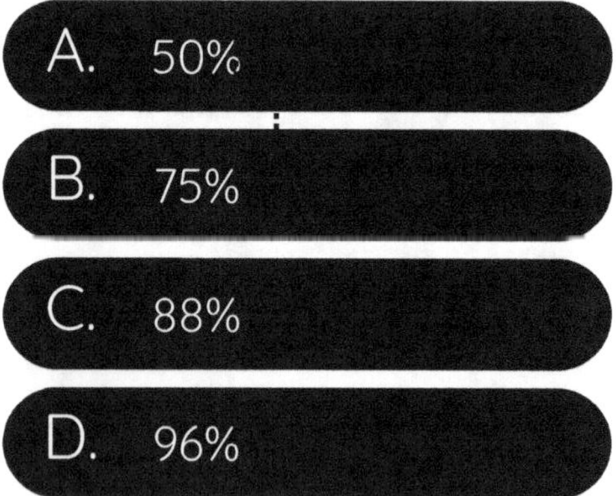

2 What percentage of cucumbers is made up of water?

A. 50%

B. 75%

C. 88%

D. 96%

Answer: Cucumbers are

D. 96% water

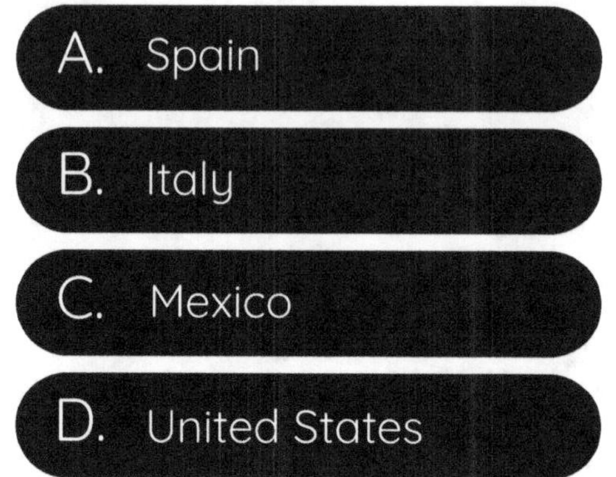

3 Where was the Caesar Salad invented?

A. Spain

B. Italy

C. Mexico

D. United States

Answer: The Caesar Salad is from

C. Mexico

4 What is the wealthiest nut?

Answer: The wealthiest nut is a cashew.

5 If I am always striving to catch up with mustard and barbecue sauce? What am I?

Answer: I am ketchup.

ROUND 1.2
QUESTIONS FOR PARENTS

6 What are the 3 names of the Rice Krispies mascots?

Answer: The names are Snap, Crackle, and Pop.

7 What is the most expensive spice in the world (by weight)?

Answer: It is saffron.

Saffron is so expensive there have been several times in history where 1g of saffron was worth more than 1g of gold.

8 What were Reese's Peanut Butter Cups originally called?

Answer: Reese's Peanut Butter Cups were originally called Penny Cups.

They used to cost 1 cent in the 1930s, and the name was later changed in 1963 when Reese's merged with Hershey.

9 Which city in Germany gives it's name to one of the USA's favorite foods, the hamburger?

Answer: It is the city of Hamburg.

It is thought that sailors who had been dealing with Russians brought back the idea of raw, shredded beef, now known as beef tartare, from the German city of Hamburg, where the term "hamburger" first appeared.

Random Fun Fact?

White chocolate is not actually chocolate. Its name is deceiving because it does not include any of the main components of real chocolate, such as cacao seeds.

Round 2

Old Slang vs New Slang

Welcome to round 2!

In this round we are going to see who knows more of the other generation's slang.

Do the kids know more of the parents' slang?

Or do the parents know more of the kids' slang?

Let's find out!

This round will have 9 slang terms that are used now that the kids should know.

And this round also has 9 slang terms that are from the past that the parents should know.

The first half of this round will be the kids guessing the old slang terms, and the second half will be the parents guessing the new slang terms.

Each question is worth 1 point.

Kids

① □
② □
③ □
④ □
⑤ □
⑥ □
⑦ □
⑧ □
⑨ □

Total Points = __________

Parents

① □
② □
③ □
④ □
⑤ □
⑥ □
⑦ □
⑧ □
⑨ □

Total Points = __________

ROUND 2.1
QUESTIONS FOR KIDS

1 What does the old slang term Da Bomb mean?

Answer: The term Da Bomb means really, really cool.

An example of this term in a sentence would be: *"That new movie is Da Bomb."*

2 What does the phrase What's the 411 mean?

Answer: The term 411 means information.

An example of this term in a sentence would be: *"Here is the 411 on tomorrow nights party."*

3 What does the phrase all that and a bag of chips mean?

Answer: All that and a bag of chips means something very special or exceptional.

An example of this in a sentence is: *"Michael Jordan is all that and a bag of chips."*

4 What does talk to the hand mean?

Answer: The term talk to the hand basically means I'm not listening and an example of this would be: *"Talk to the hand I am done with you."*

5 What does the slang word holla mean?

Answer. The word holla is basically an excited greeting. An example of this would be: *"I'll see you tomorrow, holla at me."*

6 What does the term buzz kill mean?

Answer: The term means something or someone that ruins a good feeling or kills the vibe.

An example of this in a sentence would be: *"The party was so fun, but then Uncle Joe crying was such a buzz kill."*

ROUND 2.1
QUESTIONS FOR KIDS

7 What does dibs mean?

Answer: The term dibs basically means to claim something.

An example of dibs in a sentence would be: *"I call dibs on the last slice of pizza."*

8 What does the word booyah mean?

Answer: The word booyah is used to express joy, happiness, or being elated.

An example of this in conversation would be: *"We just won the championship booyah."*

9 What does eat my shorts mean?

Answer: This phrase is an impolite dismissal or reprimand.

An example of using this term correctly would be: *"If you think I am going to do the laundry, eat my shorts."*

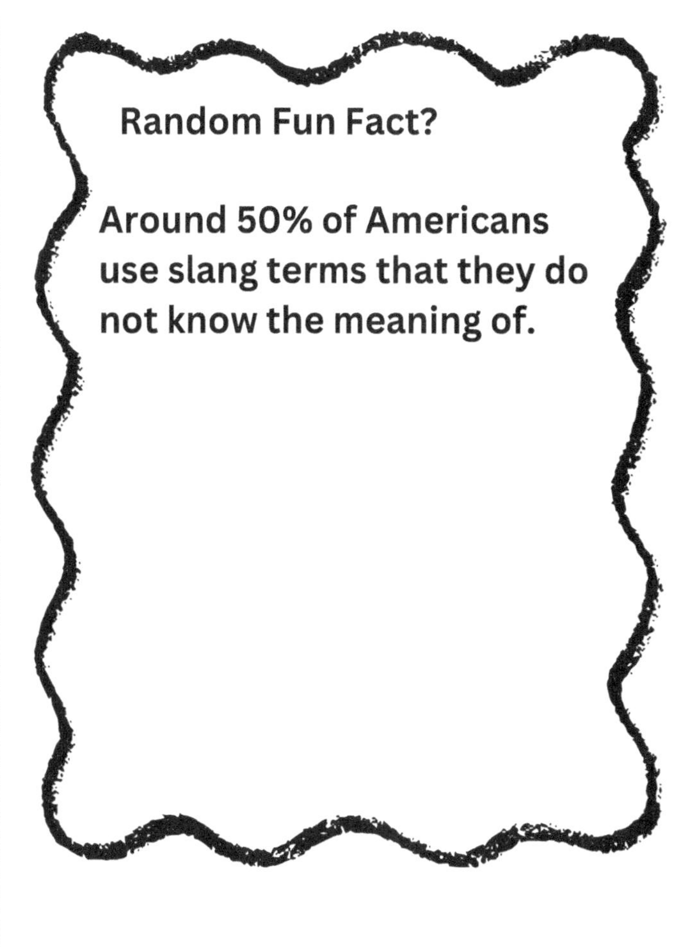

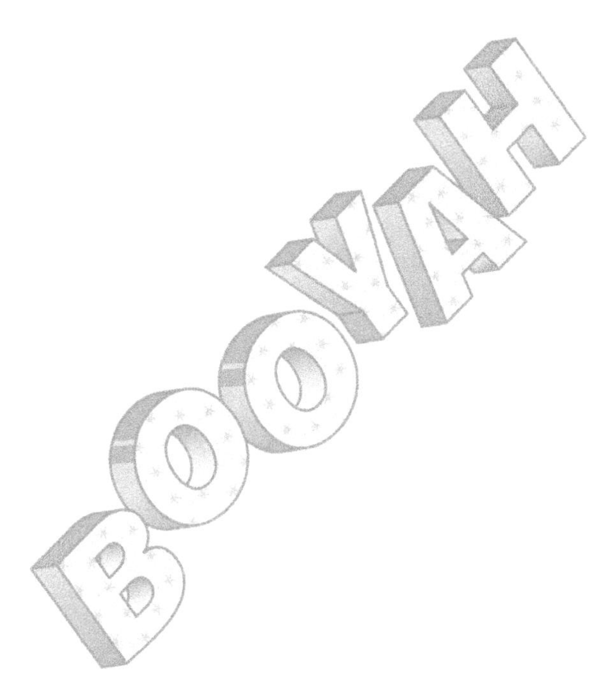

ROUND 2.2
QUESTIONS FOR PARENTS

1 What does bussin mean?

Answer: The term bussin means delicious.

An example of bussin in a sentence would be: *" That steak was bussin."*

2 What does drip mean?

Answer: Drip is stylish or cool clothing.

An example would be: *"That shirt is drip."*

Now look around; who in your family has the most drip?

3 What does okay Boomer mean?

Answer: Okay Boomer basically means an out-of-touch adult.

For this example, it takes two people so follow along: *So grandma says, "Sophie that sweater, you need to tuck it in." Granddaughter Sophie says, "Okay Boomer."*

4 What does pop off mean?

Answer: Saying pop off is a way of complimenting someone and letting them know they are so good. An example of this would be on an Instagram post a girl might comment: *"Girl, you look so good! Pop off!"*

5 What does the term slay mean?

Answer: The term slay means to do something very well.
An example of this would be someone saying: *"You slay queen."*

6 What does purr mean?

Answer: The term purr is someone expressing one's approval.
An example of this would be: *"Purr pop off girl."*

 What does sus mean?

Answer: Sus is short for suspicious. An example used in a sentence would be: *"Hey man, you are acting kind of sus."*

⑧ What does cap mean?

Answer: Cap means to lie. An example of this in a sentence would be: *"There is no way you are 6 feet tall that is cap."*
So cap now has 3 meanings

- it could be a hat
- a lid to something
- and now a lie

⑨ What does the term bet mean?

Answer: The word bet means to come to a mutual agreement.

An example in conversation would be: *Person 1 "Hey, will I see you at the game tomorrow? Person 2 Yeah, bro. Person 1 Okay, bet."*

Random Fun Fact?

46% of Americans think it's appropriate to use slang in a professional setting and 42% would use it in front of their boss.

Round 3

Geography

Welcome to round 3!

The category for this round is geography.

The style for this round will be similar to Round 1.

There will be 9 questions, and questions 8-9 will be worth 2 points.

Let's get right into it!

Kids

 1
 2
 3
 4
 5
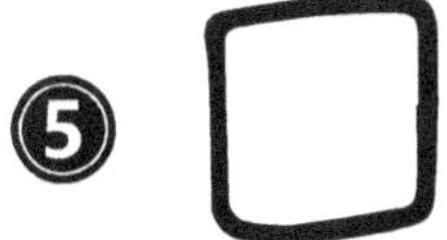 6
 7
 8
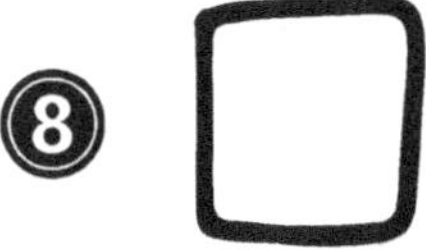 9

 Points
 Points

Parents

1 
2 
3 
4 
5 
6 
7 
8 
9 

 Points
 Points

Total Points = __________

Total Points = __________

ROUND 3.1
QUESTIONS FOR KIDS

1 On which continent is the Sahara Desert located?

A. Asia

B. South America

C. Africa

D. Europe

Answer: The Sahara Desert is in

C. Africa

2 Which nation is located further north?

A. Scotland

B. Netherlands

C. Belgium

D. Poland

Answer: It is....

A. Scotland

Scotland is located just above

England and has 790 offshore islands that reach pretty far north.

3 What is the longest river in the world?

A. Amazon River

B. Yangtze River

C. Nile River

D. Yellow River

Answer: The longest river is

C. The Nile River

The Nile River is about 4,100 miles long, which is crazy because the United States is only 2,742 miles long from the East Coast to the West Coast, making the Nile River significantly longer than the United States.

4

Answer: I am Mount Rushmore.

ROUND 3.1
QUESTIONS FOR KIDS

(5) I can create dark clouds, but they don't contain water or snow. What am I?

Answer: I am a volcano, who can make clouds out of ash.

(6) In which ocean is the Bermuda Triangle located?

Answer: It is in the Atlantic Ocean.

Now that you know about the Bermuda Triangle, beware of this mysterious place that has intrigued people for years due to many unexplained missing ships, planes, and people. Some people even believe these disappearances are due to supernatural forces.

(7) Is the correct abbreviation for Mississippi: MI or MS?

Answer: It is MS.

(8) No matter where you go, there will never be a flake identical to me. What am I?

Answer: I am a snowflake.

It's actually practically impossible to find two snowflakes with an identical shape and size.

(9) How many countries are there in the world?

Answer: There are 195 countries in the world.

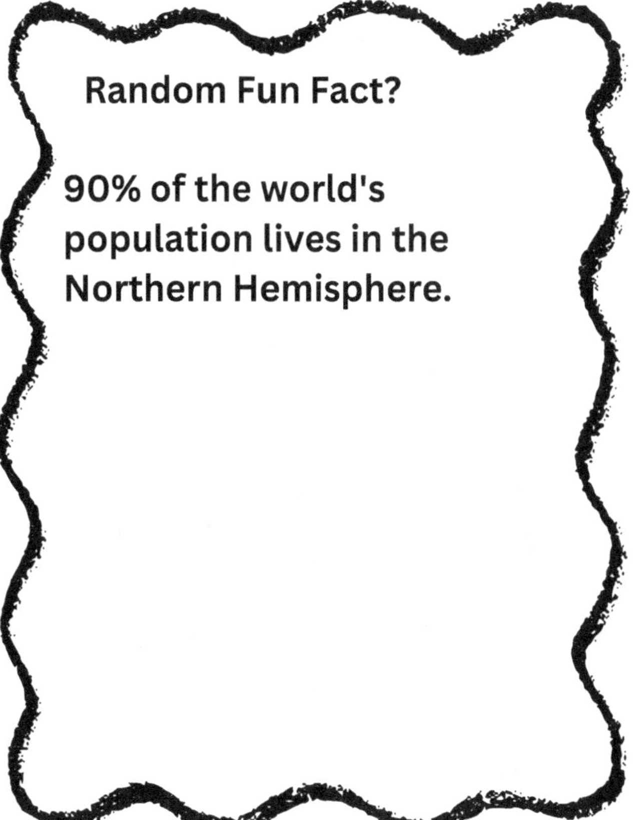

ROUND 3.2
QUESTIONS FOR PARENTS

① How tall is Mount Everest?

- **A.** 22,470 feet
- **B.** 25,751 feet
- **C.** 29,335 feet
- **D.** 32,313 feet

Answer: It is

- **C.** 29,335 feet tall

② Which river flows through London?

- **A.** River Severn
- **B.** River Trent
- **C.** River Thames
- **D.** River Great Ouse

Answer: London is home to

- **C.** River Thames

③ What is the smallest country in the world?

- **A.** Andorra
- **B.** Vatican City
- **C.** Luxembourg
- **D.** Belgium

Answer: The smallest country is

- **B.** Vatican City

I know that you might be confused and wondering how a city is a country; well, Vatican City, which covers a .17-mile radius and is home to 825 people, is a sovereign city-state that is just one-eighth the size of Central Park in New York. The pope is the head of the absolute monarchy that governs Vatican City.

④ I am a sea that touches 3 continents. What sea am I?

Answer: I am the Mediterranean Sea and I touch Africa, Asia, and Europe.

ROUND 3.2
QUESTIONS FOR PARENTS

⑤ I am made up of thousands of islands, and my top point is Mount Fuji. What country am I?

Answer: I am the country of Japan.

⑥ What is the most populated city in the world?

Answer: It is Tokyo Japan.

Which, as of today, is home to 37.4 million people.

Tokyo's population is roughly equal to the metropolitan areas of New York City and Los Angeles combined. But Tokyo is about 1/10th of the size.

⑦ What's the capital of Tennessee?

Answer: The capital is Nashville.

⑧ Where can you find oceans without water, cities without people, and forests without animals?

Answer: In a map.

⑨ What continent is the country of Malta apart of?

Answer: Malta is a part of Europe and is a small Island located in the middle of the Mediterranean Sea just south of Italy.

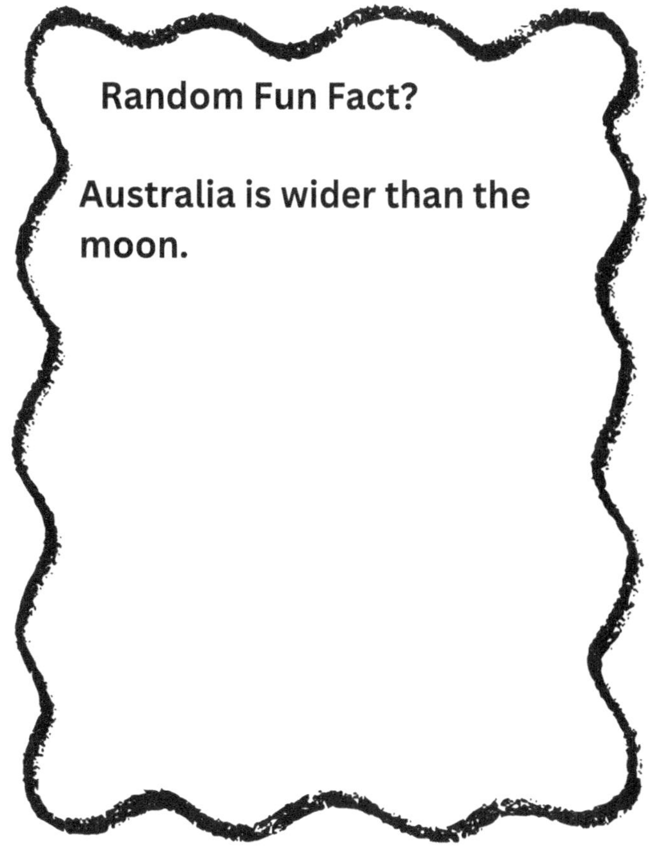

Round 4

Animals

Welcome to round 4!

This will be another standard round with 9 questions.
Questions 1-7 are worth 1 point, while questions 8-9 will be worth 2 points.

The category for this round is animals.

Let's get right into it!

Kids

1

2

3

4

5

6

7

8

 ×2 Points

9

 ×2 Points

Total Points = _______________

Parents

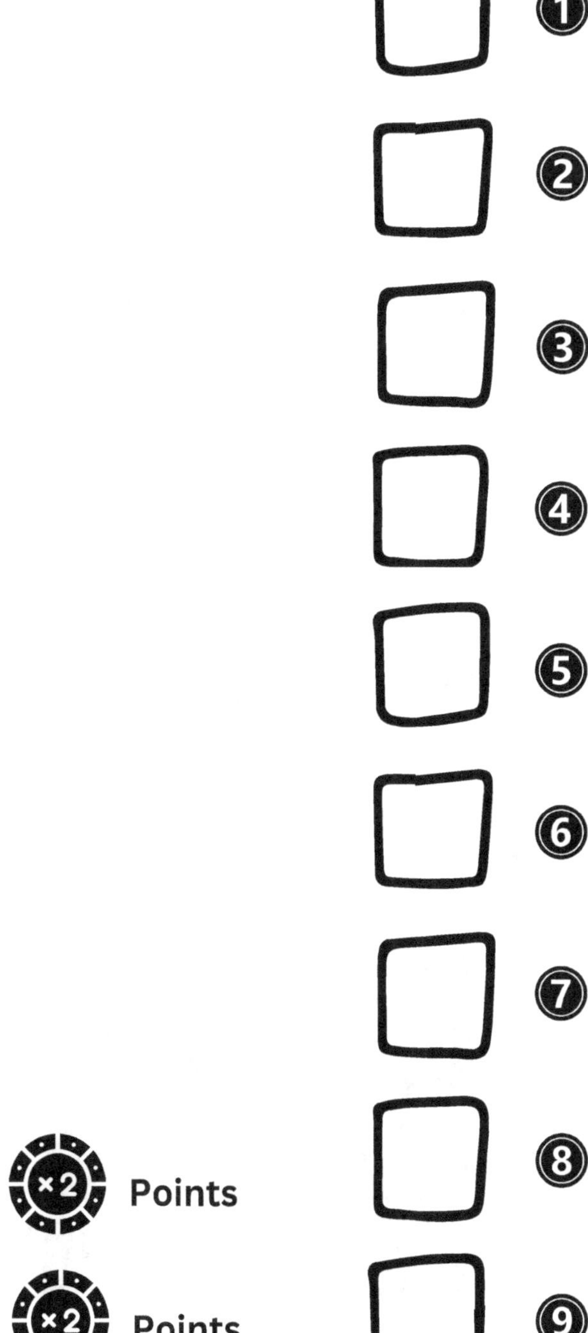

1

2

3

4

5

6

7

8

×2 Points

9

×2 Points

Total Points = _______________

ROUND 4.1
QUESTIONS FOR KIDS

1 What animal has the longest lifespan?

- **A.** Locust
- **B.** Elephant
- **C.** Blue Whale
- **D.** Giant Tortoise

Answer: It is a

D. Giant tortoise

2 How far away can a wolf smell its prey?

- **A.** .5 miles
- **B.** 2 miles
- **C.** 4 miles
- **D.** 5 miles

Answer: A wolf can detect its prey from

B. 2 miles away

3 How many times can a hummingbird flap its wings per second?

- **A.** 20 times
- **B.** 40 times
- **C.** 80 times
- **D.** 180 times

Answer: A hummingbird can flap it's wings

C. 80 times per second

4 I am the loudest insect in the world. What am I?

Answer: The loudest insect in the world is a cicada!

Cicadas are known for the loud chirping sound that males make to attract females during mating season.

⑤ I am an animal that is known to plant thousands of trees across the world. What am I?

Answer: To no surprise, this animal is a squirrel.

⑥ What species of sea creatures do the males give birth to their young?

Answer: It is a seahorse!

Seahorses are one of the few species where males carry and give birth to their offspring. How is that possible? Well, the female seahorse deposits her eggs into the male's pouch, where he fertilizes them and carries them until birth.

⑦ What animal kills the most humans every year?

Answer: The most dangerous creature to humans is a mosquito!

Mosquitos are by far the most dangerous animal in the world to humans. They cause over 700,000 human deaths a year because they transmit a number of deadly diseases, the worst of which is Malaria. So beware of mosquitoes, not sharks, lions or bears.

⑧ What percentage of animals have 2 parents raising them? (hint it's below 10%)

Answer: It is only 3%.

⑨ What is the only big cat that doesn't roar?

Answer: The only big cat that does not roar is actually the fastest cat as well. It is the cheetah.

ROUND 4.2
QUESTIONS FOR PARENTS

1 Which bird is the fastest flyer in the world?

- **A.** Peregrine Falcon
- **B.** Harpy Eagle
- **C.** Horned Sungem
- **D.** Spine Tailed Swift

Answer: The fastest flying bird is a

A. Peregrine Falcon

2 When a kangaroo is first born, it is the size of a....

- **A.** Plum
- **B.** Lima Bean
- **C.** Grape Fruit
- **D.** Watermelon

Answer: A newborn kangaroo is as big as a

B. Lima Bean

Kangaroos start out being just 1 inch in length. They continue developing in their mother's pouch until they are prepared to come out.

3 How many miles does the largest ant colony cover?

- **A.** 5 miles
- **B.** 234 miles
- **C.** 2,450 miles
- **D.** 3,700 miles

Answer: The largest known ant colony is

D. 3,700 miles

The largest known ant colony spans 3,700 miles from northern Italy to the south of France and ends on the Atlantic Coast of Spain.The colony is made up of an Argentine ant species imported from Europe called (Linepithema humile).

ROUND 4.2
QUESTIONS FOR PARENTS

④ I am a bird whose brain is smaller than my eye. What am I?

Answer: It is an ostrich which actually has the largest eyes of any land animal on Earth.

⑤ I am an insect that can turn my head 180 degrees. What am I?

Answer: This insect is a praying mantis!

⑥ What color is a spider's blood?

Answer: Spiders actually have blue blood.

⑦ What is a male duck called?

Answer: A male duck is called a drake.

⑧ Which sea creature can change its gender?

Answer: The sea creature that can change its gender is an oyster.

This is because oysters begin life as males, and most of them change their gender to become females as they mature. They can even change back from female to male. I guess whatever they feel like.

⑨ How many legs does a lobster have?

Answer: A lobster has 10 legs.

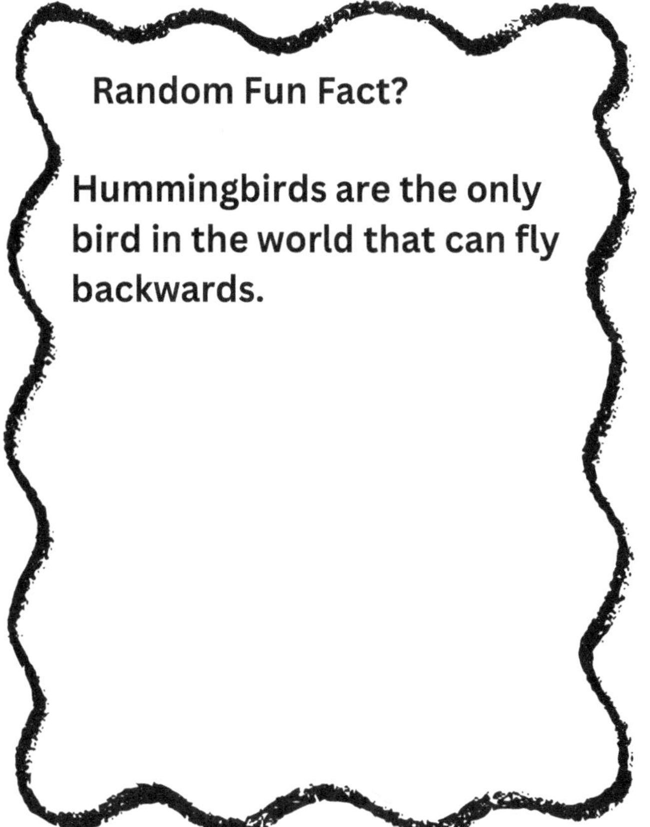

Round 5

Holidays

Welcome to round 5, the category is holidays!

This will be another standard round with 9 questions.

Questions 1-7 are worth 1 point, while questions 8-9 will be worth 2 points.

Let's get right into it!

Kids

Parents

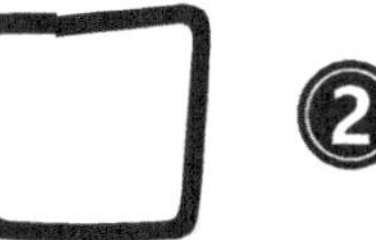

 ×2 Points

 ×2 Points

 ×2 Points

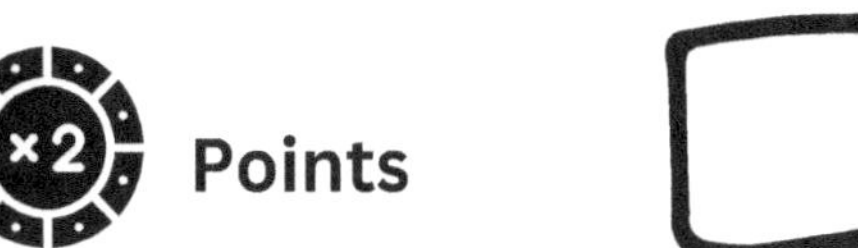 ×2 Points

Total Points = ____________

Total Points = ____________

ROUND 5.1
QUESTIONS FOR KIDS

① What snack is traditionally left out for Santa Claus?

Answer: Santa Claus is typically left with milk and cookies as a snack on Christmas Eve.

② Which Chris Van Allsburg book about a boy riding a train with other kids to the North Pole on Christmas Eve was made into a movie?

Answer: The book is *The Polar Express*!

③ What is the most recent addition to the list of U.S. federal holidays that President Joe Biden signed into law? This holiday is recognized on the 19th day of the sixth month of the year.

Answer: It is Juneteenth.

This holiday was recently implemented to celebrate the emancipation of enslaved people in the United States.

④ What are the traditional Halloween colors?

Answer: They are orange and black.

⑤ What is the famous beverage that is also known as Christmas Milk?

Answer: This beverage is eggnog.

⑥ True or false

There was turkey served at the first-ever Thanksgiving between the colonists and the pilgrims.

Answer: Even though turkeys were possibly eaten on the first Thanksgiving, it was not a common food at that time, making it unlikely that turkey was eaten at the first Thanksgiving, so even though this is not a fact, we are going to say...

The correct answer is false.

ROUND 5.1
QUESTIONS FOR KIDS

7 What is the most common New Year's Resolution?

Answer: By far, the most common New Year's Resolution is to exercise, with about 50% of New Year's Resolutions being revolved around health and fitness.

8 What day of the week is Easter on?

Answer: Easter always falls on a Sunday.

9 What does Columbus Day celebrate?

Answer: Columbus Day is a holiday remembering explorer Christopher Columbus who set sail for Asia but accidentally found America on October 12, 1492.

Random Fun Fact?

Jingle Bells" was originally a Thanksgiving song

It turns out this song by James Lord Pierpont was made for his church's Thanksgiving concert and was called "One Horse Open Sleigh." In 1857, the song was released as the Christmas song we know and love today.

Random Fun Fact?

Each year, over 400,000 illnesses are caused by spoiled holiday leftovers.

ROUND 5.2
QUESTIONS FOR PARENTS

1 True or false, 80% of parents admit to stealing Halloween candy from their children.

Answer: This is actually false; 90% of parents admit to sneaking candy from their kids' Halloween baskets.

2 What is the name of the Ballet performed during Christmas that accounts for around 50% of many dance companies' revenue?

Answer: This ballet is the Nutcracker which accounts for nearly half the annual revenue of many dance companies.

3 What American holiday is celebrated on the last Monday of May?

Answer: In America, on the last Monday of May, we celebrate Memorial Day, which is a holiday that honors the men and women who sacrificed their lives while serving in the U.S. military.

4 True or false, Saint Patrick's Day is celebrated to honor Saint Patrick's birthday.

Answer: The answer is false. Saint Patrick's Day honors the death of Saint Patrick, who was an important figure in the early church. He died on March 17, 461 A.D.

5 What time are April Fools' Day jokes supposed to stop?

Answer: If you said midnight, you are wrong. It is April Fools' custom to cease pranks at 12 pm or noon, because it is considered bad luck to play pranks in the afternoon.

6 Who was the first U.S. president to officially pardon a turkey?

Answer: In 1989, President George H.W. Bush started a tradition when he granted a Presidential Pardon to a "Fine Tom Turkey."

ROUND 5.2
QUESTIONS FOR PARENTS

⑦ What is the best-selling Christmas Song of all time?

Answer: The best-selling Christmas Song of all time and the best-selling single of all time is White Christmas by Bing Crosby.

⑧ What name is given to the Sunday before Easter?

Answer: The Sunday before Easter is called Palm Sunday.

⑨ How many national holidays are there in the U.S.?

Answer: There are 11 nationally recognized holidays in The United States.

- New Year's Day
- Martin Luther King, Jr. Day
- George Washington's Birthday (also known as Presidents Day)
- Memorial Day
- Juneteenth
- Independence Day
- Labor Day
- Columbus Day
- Veterans Day
- Thanksgiving
- Christmas

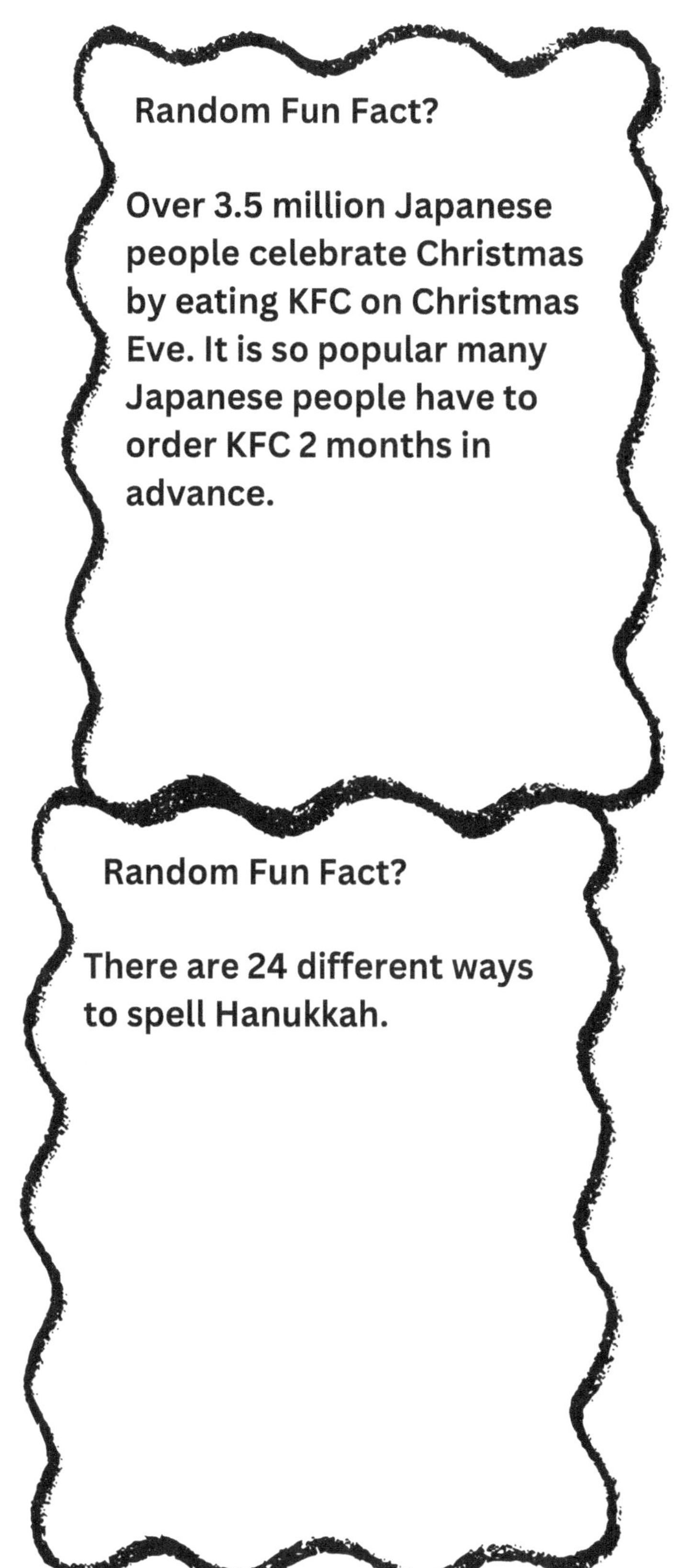

Round 6

Science

Welcome to Round 6!

The category is science!

This will be another normal round.

Questions 8-9 will be worth double the points.

Let's get into it!

Kids

 Points

 Points

Total Points = ____________

Parents

 Points
 Points

Total Points = ____________

ROUND 6.1
QUESTIONS FOR KIDS

1 What form of matter has atoms that are tightly packed together?

A. Solid

B. Liquid

C. Gas

D. Plasma

Answer: It is the

A. Solid form

2 Where are your taste buds located?

A. Tongue

B. Esophagus

C. Cheek

D. All of the above

Answer: The taste buds are located in the tongue, esophagus, and cheek, so the correct answer is...

D. All of the above

3 What is Saturn's unique characteristic compared to the other planets in our solar system?

A. Coldest

B. Oldest

C. Flattest

D. Biggest

Answer: It is the

C. Flattest planet

Saturn is so flat due to its low density and rapid rotation.

ROUND 6.1
QUESTIONS FOR KIDS

④ Which is heavier? 10 pounds of bricks or 10 pounds of feathers?

Answer: They actually both weigh the same!

⑤ It lives off of food, but it will die if you give it too much water. What is it?

Answer: It is fire.

⑥ What planet in our solar system is closest to the sun?

Answer: Mercury is the closest planet to the Sun, being 39 million miles away, while Earth is about 3 times further from the Sun, positioned 94 million miles away.

⑦ What is the name of the process that transitions a caterpillar into a butterfly?

Answer: When a caterpillar transforms into a butterfly, it is called metamorphosis.

⑧ What is the name of the tough exterior that insects have?

Answer: The hard outer covering is called an exoskeleton, and every single insect has one.

⑨ What is the process called when a gas turns into a solid?

Answer: It is called deposition. The most common example of deposition is when water vapor turns into frost. Frost can form whenever a surface, like a window, is below the freezing point of water and the air around it is humid.

ROUND 6.2
QUESTIONS FOR PARENTS

① What planet is home to the most moons?

A. Mars

B. Neptune

C. Saturn

D. Jupiter

Answer: The planet that has the most moons, with at least 76 known moons, is

D. Jupiter

② What tool is utilized to gauge the speed of wind?

A. Barometer

B. Anemometer

C. Fanometer

D. Alcometer

Answer: It is an

B. Anemometer

③ How many new species are discovered each year?

A. 100

B. 2,000

C. 11,000

D. 18,000

Answer: Every year scientist discover

D. 18,000 new species

Even after 2 centuries of research, about 18,000 new species are discovered each year, with about half of the new species being insects.

④ What can go up and down without physically moving?

Answer: It is the temperature!

ROUND 6.2
QUESTIONS FOR PARENTS

⑤ What is the most abundant gas on Earth?

Answer: The most abundant gas is nitrogen, which accounts for about 78% of all gas on Earth. The second most abundant gas is oxygen which accounts for 21% of the air on Earth.

⑥ How many elements are on the Periodic Table?

Answer: There are 118 elements on the Periodic Table.

⑦ I am behind your face and outside of your brain. What am I?

Answer: I am the scull.

⑧ What is the name of the tallest grass on Earth?

Answer: The tallest grass on Earth is, in fact, bamboo. If you asked me, I wouldn't think bamboo is a type of grass, but I guess it is.

⑨ How many bones are in the human body?

Answer: There are 206 bones in the human body.

Random Fun Fact?

You can actually die of laughing.

In rare cases, intense laughter can trigger a heart attack or cause suffocation, so be careful at comedy shows.

Round 7

Space

Welcome to Round 7!

The category is space!

This will be another normal round.

Questions 8-9 will be worth double the points.

Let's get into it!

Kids

Total Points = __________

Parents

Total Points = __________

ROUND 7.1
QUESTIONS FOR KIDS

1 Which planet has the largest ocean?

- **A.** Earth
- **B.** Mars
- **C.** Neptune
- **D.** Jupiter

Answer: The planet with the largest ocean is....

- **D.** Jupiter

Scientists speculate that if you were to go deep enough into the planet, you would eventually find an ocean. However, this ocean is quite different from Earth's ocean; it is believed that Jupiter's ocean is a 25,000-mile-deep sea of liquid metallic hydrogen.

2 The Big Dipper consist of how many stars?

- **A.** 5
- **B.** 7
- **C.** 102
- **D.** 124

Answer: There are only

- **B.** 7 stars

3 How many Earths can fit into the Sun?

- **A.** 10 thousand
- **B.** 100 thousand
- **C.** 1 million
- **D.** 1 trillion

Answer: The Sun can fit

- **C.** 1 million Earths

ROUND 7.1
QUESTIONS FOR KIDS

④ Which one of Santa's Reindeer can you see in space?

Answer: You can see Comet!

⑤ How many planets in our Solar System are surrounded by rings?

Answer: There are 4 planets with rings. Saturn, Neptune, Uranus and Jupiter.

⑥ What is the hottest planet in our Solar System?

Answer: The hottest planet in our Solar System is Venus, and it is believed that Venus reaches temperatures of up to 900° Fahrenheit.

⑦ What is the study of space called?

Answer: The study of space is called Astronomy.

⑧ How long does a Solar Eclipse last for?

Answer: A Solar Eclipse lasts for 7 and a half minutes, and a full eclipse only happens once every 18 months.

⑨ How many planets are in our Solar System?

Answer: There are 8 official planets in our Solar System. There used to be 9, but in August of 2006, the International Astronomical Union downgraded Pluto to a Dwarf Planet.

ROUND 7.2
QUESTIONS FOR PARENTS

1 How long does each season on Neptune last for?

- A. 40 years
- B. 80 years
- C. 100 years
- D. 1,000 years

Answer: Each season on Neptune only lasts....

A. 40 years

2 How far away is the nearest star from the Earth that is not the Sun?

- A. 1.2 light years away
- B. 2.4 light years away
- C. 4.2 light years away
- D. 10.1 light years away

Answer: The next nearest star is

C. 4.2 light years away

Proxima Centauri is the second closest star to Earth at 4.2 light years away. The star is over 24 trillion miles away and would take 6,300 years to reach using modern technology.

3 What color is the sunset of Mars?

- A. Yellow
- B. Red
- C. Blue
- D. Black

Answer: Mar's sunset is, in fact

C. Blue

4 What can fill up a container while taking up no space?

Answer: It is light!

ROUND 7.2
QUESTIONS FOR PARENTS

⑤ I am our Solar System's second-smallest planet; what planet am I?

Answer: Mars is the second smallest planet in our Solar System, being roughly 30% larger than the smallest planet in our Solar System, Mercury.

⑥ What is the only planet in our Solar System without a Roman deity or goddess as its name?

Answer: It is the Earth!

The word "Earth" comes from the Anglo-Saxon word erda, which means ground or soil.

⑦ What does NASA stand for?

Answer: NASA stands for National Aeronautics and Space Administration.

⑧ What was the name of the spacecraft that carried the first-ever astronauts into space?

Answer: It's name is Apollo 11.

⑨ Who was the first person to travel into space?

Answer: The first human in space was Yuri Gagarin from the Soviet Union. He went up into space for 108 minutes before a computer controlled his descent back to Earth.

Random Fun Fact?

A neutron star is so dense that 1 tsp weighs 10 million tons, which is more than the entire weight of all humans combined.

Round 8

Movies

Welcome to round 8!

This will be another normal round.

There will be 9 questions where questions 8 and 9 are worth 2 points.

The category is movies.

Let's get right into it!

Kids

 ×2 Points

 ×2 Points

Parents

Total Points = ________

Total Points = ________

ROUND 8.1
QUESTIONS FOR KIDS

1 Historically Pixar would make G rated movies; however, what was the first PG rated movie from Pixar?

A. Finding Nemo

B. The Incredibles

C. Monsters Inc.

D. Toy Story

Answer: The first ever PG movie from Pixar was

B. The Incredibles

This was because *The Incredibles* had action violence in the movie.

2 In *Harry Potter and the Half-Blood Prince* who kills Dumbledore?

A. Voldemort

B. Sirius Black

C. Bellatrix Lestrange

D. Severus Snape

Answer: Dumbledore was killed by....

D. Severus Snape

3 Who is the actress that voices Princess Elsa in *Frozen*?

A. Kristen Bell

B. Idina Menzel

C. Selena Gomez

Answer: The very talented voice actor who played Elsa in Frozen was

B. Idina Menzel

4 He has a scar on his forehead, he was sorted into the Gryffindor House and is friends with Hermione and Ron. Who is he?

Answer: This is Harry Potter.

ROUND 8.1
QUESTIONS FOR KIDS

(5) I am a district in the Hunger Games that is home to the victor of the 74th Hunger Games Katniss Everdeen. What district am I?

Answer: I am District 12.

(6) What character famously said "May the Force be with you."?

Answer: "May the force be with you" was spoken by Jedi Master Obi-Wan Kenobi to Luke Skywalker in the 1977 movie "*Star Wars: A New Hope.*"

(7) Who plays Adonis Creed in the Creed Series? Hint: he also plays Erik Killmonger in the Black Panther.

Answer: This actor is Michael B. Jordan.

(8) Which alien from the movie E.T. flies on a bike with a basket?

Answer: This famous Alien's name is E.T. The film *E.T. The Extra-Terrestrial* was made in 1982 and is one of the most famous films of all time.

(9) Who plays Hermione Granger in Harry Potter?

Answer: Hermione Granger was played by Emma Watson, who since the film has had a very successful career where she has starred in *The Perks of Being a Wallflower* in 2012, *Beauty and the Beast in 2017, Little Women* in 2019, and many other films.

Random Fun Fact?

In the movie *Now You See Me*, Isla Fisher almost actually drowned in front of the entire cast. In the underwater scene, Fisher's character was chained to the bottom of a water tank, and the chain was supposed to release easily. However, the chain got stuck, and Fisher was frantically panicking while the cast thought it was just great acting.

ROUND 8.2
QUESTIONS FOR PARENTS

1 In the Star Wars universe, how many Suns revolve around the planet of Tatooine, which is Luke Skywalker's home?

A. 2

B. 52

C. 347

D. 1,004

Answer: There are......

A. 2 Planets

2 Which Top Gun actor didn't vomit while filming in fighter jets?

A. Tom Cruise

B. Val Kilmer

C. John Stockwell

D. Anthony Edwards

Answer: The only actor who didn't vomit while in the fighter jets was..

D. Anthony Edwards

Anthony played Goose.

3 In the 2009 Avatar, how long could it take to render a single CGI frame (which is only 1/24th of a second)?

A. 47 seconds

B. 47 minutes

C. 47 hours

Answer: Some individual frames reportedly took up to

C. 47 hours

It took so long due to the film's complex CGI. Avatar had 100's of CGI artists and technicians that worked for years on this movie, which was a major factor in the movie's success.

ROUND 8.2
QUESTIONS FOR PARENTS

④ I played Danny Zuko in the movie *Grease*. Who am I?

Answer: I am John Travolta.

⑤ This movie was made in 1984, has a giant marshmallow and ghosts in it. What movie is this?

Answer: This movie is *Ghostbusters*.

⑥ At the beginning of *The Matrix*, what color pill does Neo take?

Answer: In the first Matrix Movie, Neo, the main character, had a choice to make. He could take a red pill that would allow him to see the truth about the Matrix, or he could take a blue pill and continue experiencing his allusion. He chose the red pill and saw the true oppressive nature of the Matrix.

⑦ "You're gonna need a bigger boat." is a famous line from which movie?

Answer: This quote comes from the film *Jaws* and is spoken by Chief Brody moments after the shark appears behind the orca.

⑧ What is the highest-grossing movie of all time? (when taking inflation into account)

Answer: The highest-grossing movie, when taking inflation into account, is *Gone With The Wind*. The movie was released in 1939, and it grossed $393.4 million in 1939 dollars, plus $88 million across the International Box Office. Adjusted to inflation, this would have grossed around $3.44 billion in today's money.

⑨ What is the highest-grossing movie of all time if you do not take inflation into account?

Answer: The highest-grossing movie of all time (not taking inflation into account) is *Avengers Endgame* which grossed a total of 2.8 billion dollars in global revenue.

Round 9

Who is Most Likely

Welcome to round 9! This round is kind of a bonus chapter to switch up the pace and give you some variety. Playing regular trivia can get a little stale after a while, which is why we try to switch up the style every few rounds.

In this round, you will ask a question, and then the group must share who they think is "most likely to" and provide an explanation for why.

Let's do a practice question.

Who is the most likely to finish eating first?

Point to the person you think is most likely to finish eating first in 3 2 1 go.

So now that you understand...

Whatever team receives the least amount of nominations wins the round.

There will be 21 questions, each worth 1 point.

If the people on team parents gets the least nominations, team parents win. If the people on team kids gets the least nominations, then team kids win.

Okay, so I hope you get the rules; after 3 2 1 go, everyone points at who they think. Good luck!

Kids

Parents

1		12	
2		13	
3		14	
4		15	
5		16	
6		17	
7		18	
8		19	
9		20	
10		21	
11			

Total Points = _________

ROUND 9.1
QUESTIONS FOR EVERYONE

1 Who is the most likely to sleep past an alarm clock?

2 Who is most likely to put their shirt on backwards?

3 Who is most likely to have to go pee on a road trip?

4 Who is the most likely to get sick?

5 Who is the least likely to get sick?

6 Who is the messiest?

7 Who is the most likely to stay up all night?

8 Who is most likely to go a week without changing their clothes?

9 Who is the most likely to come up with an invention?

10 Who is most likely to take a super long shower?

11 Who is most likely to become president?

12 Who is the funniest?

13 Who is most likely to live in a different country one day?

14 Who is most likely to live through a Zombie Apocalypse?

15 Who is most likely to lose their hotel room key?

16 Who is most likely to use the last of the toilet paper and not replace the roll?

17 Who is most likely to go to space?

18 Who is most likely to write a best-selling book?

19 Who is most likely to have an imaginary friend?

20 Who is most likely to sleep in class?

21 Who is most likely to get scared and scream in a haunted house?

Thank you so much
for reading our book

If you have 30 seconds we would really appreciate a review

SCAN ME

Round 10

Music

Welcome to round 10!

This round is going to be a normal one where there are 9 questions each, with questions 8 and 9 being worth 2 points.

The category for this round is music.

Let's get right into it!

Kids

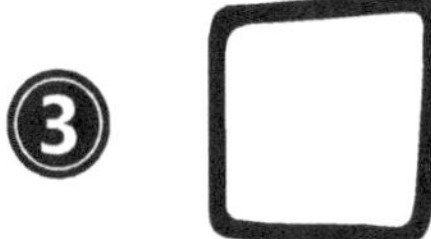

 Points

 Points

Total Points = ______

Parents

ROUND 10.1
QUESTIONS FOR KIDS

1 What was Adele's 2015 album called?

A. 19

B. 21

C. 25

D. 29

Answer: The name of Adele's 2015 album is

C. 25

Adele's album titles reflect the age she was when she wrote them. So her 2015 album was named 25 because she wrote it when she was 25, but the album was not released until she was 27.

2 Who has the most number 1 hit singles of all time?

A. The Beatles

B. Elvis Presley

C. Michael Jackson

Answer: The artist/ group with the most number 1 singles is

A. The Beatles

As of today, the Beatles hold the record for the most number 1 songs in history. They were able to get 20 singles to hit number 1, all within the span of 8 years.

3 Who made the song called "Two Lanes of Freedom", which features Taylor Swift and Keith Urban?

A. George Strait

B. Luke Bryan

C. Kenny Chesney

D.

Answer: It was

C. Kenny Chesney

ROUND 10.1
QUESTIONS FOR KIDS

④ My nickname is Mr. Worldwide, I am a famous artist who has made songs by the name of "Timber", "Fireball", and "Feel This Moment." Who am I?

Answer: I am Pitbull.

⑤ I am known as the "King of Pop" and have made many hit songs such as "Thriller", "Beat It", and "Bad". Who am I?

Answer: The "King of Pop" and one of the most influential figures of the 20th century is Michael Jackson.

⑥ Who wrote the song, "We Don't Talk Anymore"?

Answer: "We Don't Talk Anymore" was written by Charlie Puth.

⑦ How many members of One Direction were there?

Answer: Before breaking up, One Direction was composed of 5 members: Niall Horan, Liam Payne, Harry Styles, Louis Tomlinson, and Zayn Malik.

⑧ Who sang the 2014 hit single "Chandelier"?

Answer: "Chandelier" is a song by Australian singer and songwriter Sia, whose real name is Sia Kate Isobelle Furler.

⑨ The "Despacito" remix in 2017 hit number 1 on the U.S. charts for 16 straight weeks. Which popular Canadian artist was featured on the remix?

Answer: Justin Bieber was the featured artist on the "Despacito" remix. The collaboration ended up boosting the song to the top position of the Billboard Hot 100 singles chart for 16 straight weeks. This tied the record for the longest streak at the top position previously held by Mariah Carey and Boyz II Men's single "One Sweet Day."

ROUND 10.2
QUESTIONS FOR PARENTS

1 What was the best-selling United States album in the year 1970?

> A. "Let It Be" by the Beatles

> B. "Paranoid" by Black Sabbath

> C. "Bridge Over Troubled Water" by Simon and Garfunkel

> D. "Led Zeppelin III" by Led Zeppelin

Answer: The Bestselling album in the year 1970 was....

> C. **"Bridge Over Troubled Water"**

In 1970, Simon and Garfunkel's album sold over 25 million copies, which is almost double the amount of the second best-selling album of the year "Led Zeppelin III", which produced 13 million sales.

2 What year did Michael Jackson release the "Bad" album?

> A. 1980

> B. 1985

> C. 1987

Answer: Michael Jackson released "Bad" on August 31st of...

> C. 1987

3 Which of the following artists has had the most songs hit the top 100 charts?

> A. Bruno Mars

> B. Drake

> C. Justin Bieber

> D. Eminem

Answer: It is...

> A. Bruno Mars

4 I am the producer who founded the company Beats Electronics, and I also signed Eminem in 1998 to the label Aftermath. Who am I?

Answer: I am Dr. Dre, a producer who helped some of the biggest rappers launch their careers, such as Snoop Dog and Eminem.

ROUND 10.2
QUESTIONS FOR PARENTS

5 What was Nirvana's most commercially successful song?

Answer: By far, Nirvana's most successful song was "Smells Like Teen Spirit" which was the first single from their hit second album "Nevermind".

6 What song was released as the theme song for *Rocky III* (1982)?

Answer: It was the "Eye of the Tiger."

7 What American singer/songwriter made the hit "Man in Black" (1971)?

Answer: It was Johnny Cash.

8 What is the name of the legendary 1979 number 1 hit single by Gloria Gaynor?

Answer: The Legendary hit was "I Will Survive", sung by Gloria Gaynor was actually not written by her; the song was written by Freddie Perren and Dino Fekaris. Since they were without a singer when they created "I Will Survive," they decided the next diva to find them would perform the song. Gloria Gaynor turned out to be the lucky woman.

9 Which member of the Beatles wrote 'We All Stand Together" for the movie *Rupert and the Frog Song*?

Answer: It was Paul McCartney who was one of the two lead singers for the Beatles.

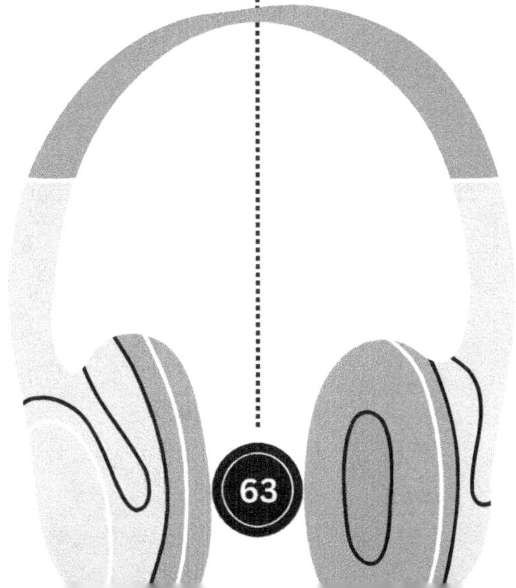

Round 11

Celebrities

Welcome to round 11!

This round is going to be a normal one where there are 9 questions each, with questions 8 and 9 being worth 2 points.

The category for this round is celebrities.

Let's get right into it!

Kids

 Points

 Points

Parents

 Points

 Points

Total Points = ____________________

1 Who is the oldest Kardashian/Jenner sister?

- A. Kim Kardashian
- B. Kourtney Kardashian
- C. Khloe Kardashian
- D. Kendall Jenner

Answer: The Oldest Sister by 2 years is

B. Kourtney Kardashian

She is two years older than Kim Kardashian, who is the second oldest of the 5 sisters.

2 Zendaya competed on which reality show?

- A. Dancing with the Stars
- B. Survivor
- C. American Idol
- D. Jeopardy

Answer: In 2013, Zendaya competed on season 16 of....

A. Dancing With The Stars

She came in second place.

3 Where did Prince William meet Kate Middleton?

- A. Family connections
- B. At a dinner party
- C. St. Andrews University
- D. Windsor Castle

Answer: The pair first met at....

C. St. Andrews University

④ I won Mr. Olympia 6 years in a row, and I am considered by many as the greatest bodybuilder of all time, I have also starred in the movie "Terminator" and served as the 38th governor of California.

Who am I?

Answer: I am Arnold Schwarzenegger.

⑤ I slapped Chris Rock in the face.

Who am I?

Answer: During the 2022 Oscars ceremony, Will Smith slapped Chris Rock on national television.

⑥ Who wrote the book "To Kill a Mockingbird"?

Answer: It was Harper Lee.

⑦ What city was the rapper Drake born in?

Answer: Drake was born in Toronto, Ontario.

⑧ Who is the husband of actress Mila Kunis?

Answer: Mila Kunis married Ashton Kutcher, and they have a genuine Hollywood love story. They met on Set of "That 70's Show" where they played on-and-off couple, Jackie Burkhart and Michael Kelso. They actually never ended up dating until 15 years later.

⑨ Who starred as Forrest Gump in the 1994 movie "Forrest Gump"?

Answer: Tom Hanks starred as Forrest Gump.

ROUND 11.2
QUESTIONS FOR PARENTS

1 How many children does Angelina Jolie have?

A. 1

B. 3

C. 6

D. 10

Answer: Angelina Jolie has

C. 6 Kids

She has 6 kids, 4 of whom she adopted before she gave birth to her twins Knox and Vivienne in 2008.

2 According to Forbes, which actress earned the most money in 2019?

A. Angelina Jolie

B. Scarlett Johansson

C. Emily Blunt

D. Jennifer Lawrence

Answer: After earning an 8 figure paycheck for her role in the "Black Widow" and collecting 35 Million in back-end payments from "Avengers Endgame", the highest-paid actor in 2018 was

B. Scarlett Johansson

3 What is the name of Michelle Obama's memoir?

A. Untamed

B. Forward

C. Hold Still

D. Becoming

Answer: The name of Michelle Obama's memoir is

D. Becoming

She uses the word becoming to sum up her journey of always evolving.

④ I am a basketball player who met Kim Jong Un and played for the Chicago Bulls in the 90's.

Who am I?

Answer: I am Dennis Rodman.

⑤ I am Justin Bieber's wife.

Who am I?

Answer: I am Hailey Bieber.

⑥ Which famous businessman/ entrepreneur named his son X AE A-12?

Answer: It was Elon Musk, and the name is pronounced like this "X ash A 12."

⑦ Who is the highest-earning author of all time?

Answer: J.K. Rowling, the author of the Harry Potter series, is the richest author in the world, with a net worth of 1 billion dollars.

⑧ Which famous actor was the former mayor of Carmel, California?

Answer: On April 8, 1986, Clint Eastwood was elected mayor of Carmel, but after his two-year term was over, he did not run for a second term.

⑨ In 2019, who did Forbes recognize as the youngest "self-made billionaire ever"?

Answer: Due to her Business, Kylie Cosmetics, Kylie Jenner was the youngest self-made Billionaire, achieving a net worth of over 1 billion dollars at the age of 21.

Round 12

Welcome to round 12!

It will be another normal round again; however, we have an interesting category for this chapter.

This round is going to be miscellaneous questions.

With that being said, let's get into it!

Kids

1
2
3
4
5
6
7
8
9

 **Points**

 **Points**

Total Points = ___________

Parents

Total Points = ___________

ROUND 12.1
QUESTIONS FOR KIDS

1 According to Japanese legend, what kind of origami must be folded 1,000 times in order for a sick person to heal?

> **A.** Frog

> **B.** Panda

> **C.** Fish

> **D.** Crane

Answer: It is a

> **D.** Crane

According to a Japanese legend, anyone who folds 1,000 origami cranes will recover from illness because the crane is said to have a thousand-year lifespan.

2 What is the most kids ever born to one mother?

> **A.** 27

> **B.** 43

> **C.** 69

Answer: From 1725 to 1765, the wife of Feodor Vassilyev a peasant from Shuya, Russia, gave birth to

> **C.** 69 kids

20 singles, 6 twins, 7 triplets, and 4 sets of quadruplets.

3 What animal travels the furthest for migration every year?

> **A.** Ice Pigeon

> **B.** Arctic Tern

> **C.** Blue Whale

Answer: The furthest migration is made by the

> **B.** Arctic Tern

The Arctic Tern is a small bird known for its speed and lengthy migration from the South Pole to the North Pole.

ROUND 12.1
QUESTIONS FOR KIDS

(4) Even though I'm lighter than a feather, few can hold me for 7 minutes straight.

What am I?

Answer: I am your breath.

(5) I'll always come, but I won't show up today.

What am I?

Answer: Tomorrow always comes but never arrives today.

(6) Who painted the Mona Lisa?

Answer: The painter was Leonardo da Vinci.

(7) Pickles start out as which vegetable?

Answer: A pickle starts out as a cucumber before the fermentation process turns the cucumber into a pickle.

(8) What makes warm currents develop in the Pacific Ocean every 3-7 years, resulting in odd weather patterns around the world?

Answer: An El Niño causes all of this.

(9) How many oceans are there in the world?

Answer: There are 5 oceans which are connected and actually one huge body of water. The 5 oceans in order from smallest to largest, are the....

Arctic Ocean

Southern Ocean

Indian Ocean

Atlantic Ocean

Pacific Ocean

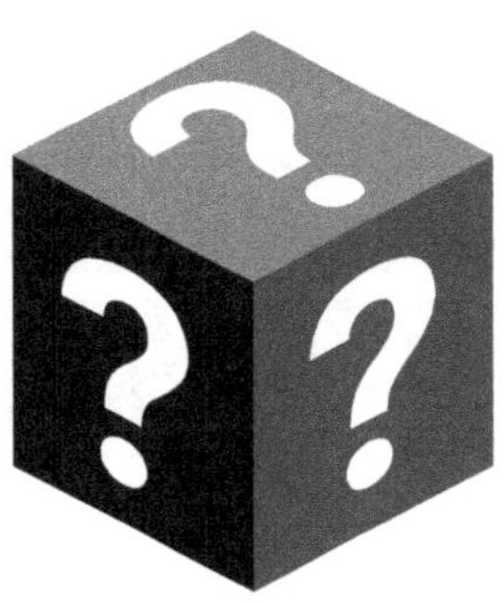

ROUND 12.2
QUESTIONS FOR PARENTS

① There is a common saying be back in a jiffy. A jiffy is actually a real unit of time. How long is a jiffy?

> **A.** 1 trillionth of a second

> **B.** 1 tenth of a second

> **C.** 5 seconds

> **D.** 5 minutes

Answer: A jiffy is

> **A.** 1 trillionth of a second

This is the time required for light to move 1 centimeter.

② Every king in a deck of cards has a mustache, except for?

> **A.** King of Spades

> **B.** King of Hearts

> **C.** King of Diamonds

> **D.** King of Clubs

Answer: It is....

> **B.** The King of Hearts

Answer: The reason for this is very interesting.

Each of the kings represents something.

The King of Diamonds represents corruption of money.

The King of Clubs represents conflict in war.

The King of Spades represents death.

So these 3 kings all have mustaches, which represent them hiding things and being deceitful.

While the King of Hearts represents love, empathy, and purity, which is why the King of Hearts is clean-shaven; he is open and has nothing to hide.

ROUND 12.2
QUESTIONS FOR PARENTS

3 How much did the most expensive cow ever sell for?

A. $ 100,700

B. $ 300,500

C. $ 504,000

D. 1.3 million dollars

Answer: In 1985 there was a cow that was bought for

D. 1.3 million dollars

This cow likely served as a matriarch for a lineage of star milk producers.

4 I am very light, yet no one can throw me far.

What am I?

Answer: I am a feather.

5 I'll always come, but I won't show up today. What am I?

Answer: Tomorrow always comes but never arrives today.

6 What is the unit of currency in Russia?

Answer: It is a rubble and 1 US dollar equals 90 Russian rubbles.

7 How many colors are there in a rainbow?

Answer: There are 7 colors: red, orange, yellow, green, blue, indigo, and violet.

8 Name one of the differences between Amphibians and Reptiles?

Answer: Reptiles hatch from eggs that have a protective outer layer, while Amphibians lay jelly-like eggs that you can see through. Reptiles have scales and their skin is dry. Amphibians do not, and their skin is often moist. Also, Amphibians can breathe through their skin. If you said any of these you are right.

9 Brazil's flag consist of which 4 colors?

Answer: The 4 colors are green, yellow, blue, and white.

Round 13

Who Said?

Welcome to Round 13!

In this round, we are going to play a fun little game called Who Said?

This game is pretty similar to regular trivia; however, all the questions will be who-said questions instead of having multiple choice, riddles, and short answer questions.

Hope you enjoy!

There will be 10 questions worth 1 point for each of the kids and parents.

Let's get started!

Kids

Total Points = ________

Parents

Total Points = ________

ROUND 13.1
QUESTIONS FOR KIDS

1 Who said: "That's one small step for a man, one giant leap for mankind."

Answer: It was Neil Armstrong.

2 Which famous international soccer/ footballer player said, "I see myself as the best footballer in the world. If you don't believe you are the best, then you will never achieve all that you are capable of."

Answer: It was Cristiano Ronaldo.

3 Who said "The British are coming."

Answer: It was Paul Revere when he was warning the colonists that the British were coming to invade.

4 Which actor famously said, "I'll be back." and "Hasta la vista baby."

Answer: It was Arnold Schwarzenegger in The Terminator series. These two Arnold quotes are some of the most iconic and recognizable quotes in Hollywood history.

5 Who said, "I have a dream that my four little children will one day live in a nation where they will not be judged by the color of their skin but by the content of their character."

Answer: It was Martin Luther King Jr.

6 Which one of the Founding Fathers said, "Well done is better than well said."

Answer: This was said by Benjamin Franklin.

7 Which well-known blind and deaf woman said, "The best and most beautiful things in the world cannot be seen or even touched — they must be felt with the heart."

Answer: It was Hellen Keller.

ROUND 13.1
QUESTIONS FOR KIDS

8 Which iconic baseball player said, "Never let the fear of striking out keep you from playing the game."

Answer: This was said by Babe Ruth.

9 Which movie character said, "Life is like a box of chocolates; you never know what you're gonna get."

Answer: It was Forrest Gump whom Tom Hanks played in the 1994 film "Forrest Gump."

10 Which Greek philosopher said, "The unexamined life is not worth living."

Answer: The phrase is credited to the Ancient Greek philosopher Socrates during his trial, in which he was executed for opposing Greek culture's ideas and beliefs and for influencing the youth with his ideas.

Random Fun Fact?

The oldest known quote was made my Homer in 11,000 BC. The quote was "Be still my heart. You have known worse than this."

Random Fun Fact?

Socrates did not write any of his books or texts.
Most of the information we know about him comes from the writings of his students. Socrates's students were so inspired by his teachings that they sought to preserve and share his ideas.

ROUND 13.2
QUESTIONS FOR PARENTS

① Which musician who was murdered said, "Life is what happens when you are busy making other plans."

Answer: This was said by John Lennon.

② Which Roman general said, "I came, I saw, I conquered."

Answer: It was Julius Caesar.

③ Which American tech business icon said, "Stay hungry. stay foolish."

Answer: It was Steve Jobs.

④ Which famous nonacademic philosopher from India said, "Live as if you were to die tomorrow. Learn as if you were to live forever."

Answer: This was said by Gandhi.

⑤ Which American inventor said, "Genius is one percent inspiration and ninety-nine percent perspiration."

Answer: It was Thomas Edison.

⑥ Which boxer said, "I am the greatest. I said that before I knew, I was."

Answer: It was Muhammad Ali.

⑦ Which talkshow host from Mississippi said, "If you look at what you have in life, you'll always have more. If you look at what you don't have in life, you'll never have enough."

Answer: It was Oprah Winfrey.

ROUND 13.2
QUESTIONS FOR PARENTS

8 Which Indian catholic nun said, "Spread love wherever you go. Let no one ever come to you without leaving happier."

Answer: Mother Teresa said this.

9 Which American pioneer of the animation and film industry said, "The way to get started is to quit talking and start doing."

Answer: Walt Disney said this.

10 Which actor famously said, "I am the king of the World!"

Answer: After getting a ticket onto the boat in the 1997 movie Titanic, Leonardo DiCaprio goes to the front of the ship and exclaims, "I am the King of the World!"

Random Fun Fact?

Walt Disney's first animation studio went bankrupt.

Within a year, Walt Disney's first studio, Laugh-o-Gram, was forced to file for bankruptcy.

Random Fun Fact?

People forget 50-80% of what they've learned after one day and 97-98% after a month.

Round 14

War

Welcome to round 14!

This will be another normal round.
There are 9 questions with questions 8 and 9 are worth 2 points.

The category is war.

Good luck!

Kids

 Points

 Points

Total Points = ____________

Parents

Total Points = ____________

ROUND 14.1
QUESTIONS FOR KIDS

1 What was the deadliest war for United States soldiers?

> **A.** World War II

> **B.** American Civil War

> **C.** World War I

> **D.** Vietnam War

Answer: The deadliest war for U.S. soldiers was

> **D.** The Civil War

There were 620,000 American casualties in the Civil War.

2 Which of the following people had significant roles in both World Wars?

> **A.** Adolf Hitler

> **B.** Woodrow Wilson

> **C.** Winston Churchill

> **D.** Benito Mussolini

Answer: It was

> **C.** Winston Churchill

Churchill served in the War Council, as First Lord of the Admiralty, and as Minister of Munitions during World War I. In World War II, Churchill again served as First Lord of the Admiralty. Then, in the midst of World War II (May 1940), he was appointed Prime Minister of Great Britain.

3 What is the longest-lasting war in history?

> **A.** Hundred Years War

> **B.** Reconquista

> **C.** World War II

> **D.** Roman-Germanic War

Answer on the next page!

Answer: The longest war ever was

B. The Reconquista

The war lasted 774 years from 718-1492, with approximately 7 million deaths. This was a war between the Christian Kingdoms and the Muslim Moors over the Iberian Peninsula. The Reconquista ended in 1492 when the last Muslim stronghold fell to the Catholic Monarchs of Spain.

④ The 1936 Spanish Civil War was fought in Spain. What two countries fought in this war?

Answer: It was a civil war, so it was Spain vs Spain.

⑤ I am the conqueror who has conquered more land than anyone else in history. Who am I?

Answer: Genghis Khan was the greatest conqueror of all time due to the series of conquests and campaigns he led, capturing 11-12 million miles of territory (which is roughly the size of Africa).

⑥ What was the bloodiest battle of the U.S. Civil War?

Answer: It was the Battle of Gettysburg, which left nearly 52,000 men killed, wounded, or missing in action.

⑦ What U.S. state is the Tomb of the Unknown Soldier located in?

Answer: The Tomb of the Unknown Soldier is located in Virginia.

⑧ What is the blade attached to the end of a gun for hand-to-hand combat called?

Answer: It is a Bayonet.

⑨ The Hundred Years War was between which 2 European countries?

Answer: The Hundred Years War, which lasted from 1337 to 1453, was essentially a sequence of battles between England and France that started because of the inability to name a king.

1 What war is known as being "The war to end all wars"?

- **A.** World War I
- **B.** The Civil War
- **C.** World War II
- **D.** War of 1812

Answer: The war to end all wars was

- **A.** World War I

2 What general during the American Revolutionary War originally fought for the American Continental Army but shifted his allegiance to the British Army?

- **A.** William Howe
- **B.** Horatio Gates
- **C.** Benedict Arnold

Answer: The American traitor was

- **C.** Benedict Arnold

In 1799, after negotiating with the British, Benedict Arnold agreed to hand over the American station at West Point in exchange for cash and command of a British Army. Since then, he has been notoriously recognized as an American traitor.

3 Which of the following was a device used by Ancient Roman Warships to board enemy ships?

- **A.** Gladius
- **B.** Karabella
- **C.** Pulwar
- **D.** Corvus

Answer: This Roman device was a

- **D.** Corvus

The Corvus was basically a bridge that could be deployed from the Roman ship onto an enemy ship.

ROUND 14.2
QUESTIONS FOR PARENTS

4 Sometimes I expand, sometimes I shrink. I am gained in conquest and lost in defeat. I signify your downfall and your success. The more of me you have, the more things you have the ability to do. What am I?

Answer: I am power.

5 I am the man who dropped the first atomic bomb. Who am I?

Answer: On August 6, 1945, Paul Tibbet dropped the first atomic bomb on Hiroshima. He retired from the Air Force 20 years later and passed away in 2007.

6 Which war did the U.S. enter into between June 25, 1950, and July 27, 1953?

Answer: It was the Korean War.

7 Which French commander and emperor was exiled twice and able to conquer large parts of Europe during the early 19th century?

Answer: It was Napoleon Bonaparte.

8 What century were guns first used in war?

Answer: Firearms were first used in the 14th century; however, they were not very effective, and throughout the 14th and 15th centuries, guns and crossbows continued to be used side by side. The first battles actually to be decided by firearms were believed to be fought between French and Spanish troops in the Battle of Marignano during the early 16th century.

9 The youngest American service member in World War II was how old?

Answer: Calvin Graham, at 12 years old, was the youngest service member in World War II. Graham lied about his age when he joined the Navy, and it wasn't until after he was injured in combat that his true age was revealed.

Round 15

Decades

Welcome to Round 15!

This will be a relatively normal round.

The category is decades, and we will be asking 2 questions from each decade, starting from the 70's to the 2010's. Each question is worth 1 point.

Good luck!

Kids

① 

②

③ 

④

⑤ 

⑥ 

⑦ 

⑧ 

⑨ 

⑩ 

Total Points = ________

Parents

①

②

③

④

⑤

⑥

⑦

⑧

⑨

⑩

Total Points = ________

ROUND 15.1
QUESTIONS FOR KIDS

1 What 1970s girl's fashion trend featured pants with a flare at the bottom?

Answer: It was bellbottoms, and this 70s trend has recently been making a comeback in modern fashion.

2 Which American president served the longest term in the 70s?

Answer: Richard Nixon served more time than anyone else in the 70's. His first term was from 1969 to 1973; then, he was re-elected for a second term before resigning on August 9, 1974.

3 What is the name of the Washington Volcano that in 1980 had the deadliest eruption in American history?

Answer: It is Mount St. Helens and its volcanic eruption claimed 57 lives and caused extensive damage to the surrounding landscape, leaving behind a massive crater.

4 Which NFL team won the most Super Bowls in the 80s?

A. Dallas Cowboys

B. Pittsburgh Steelers

C. San Francisco 49ners

D. Miami Dolphins

Answer: The most successful team in the 80s lead by Joe Montana and winning 4 super bowls was

C. San Fancisco 49ners

5 What was the most popular video game console in the 1990s?

Answer: In the 90's the Sony PlayStation sold more units than any other gaming console, with 102 million consoles sold throughout the decade.

6 In 1996 the first-ever cloned sheep. was created. What was its name?

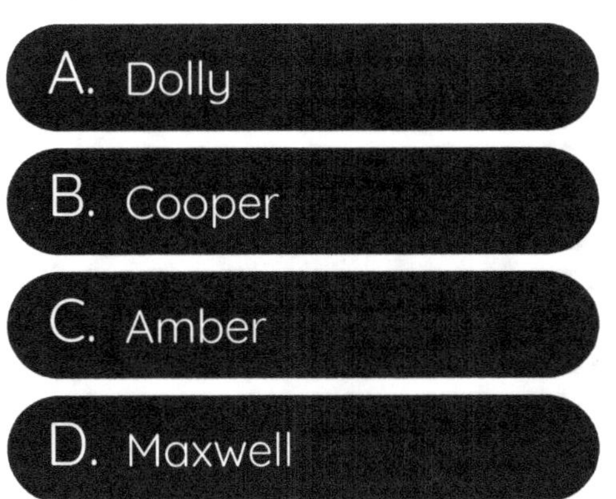

Answer: The first cloned sheep's name was

7 In 2004, Harvard dorm room students created a social media platform designed to connect college students. It has since become one of the largest social media platforms in the world. What is the name of this platform?

Answer: Facebook, now known as Meta, was created by Mark Zuckerberg and his 3 roommates in their dorm room at Harvard.

8 Which century is the 2000s in?

Answer: It is the 21st century and is not called the 20th century because, according to the calendar we use, the 1st century included the years 1-100 (there was no century zero), and the 2nd century included years 101-200.

9 What was the most popular social media platform of the 2010s?

Answer: With over 1 billion active users, Instagram was the most-used social media network of the decade.

10 What country was the 2018 Winter Olympics held in?

Answer: Taking place in Pyeongchang, South Korea, the 2018 Olympics was the first Winter Olympics ever hosted in Asia.

70's

① What year was the first Apple computer released?

Answer: The first Apple computer was released on April 1, 1976, and sold for $666.66, which is equivalent to around $3,500 today.

70's

② What was the popular 70s hairstyle that involved mid-length to long hair, brushed back and outward at the sides?

Answer: It was the feathered look, which is arguably the most popular hairstyle of the 70s.

80's

③ What doll was really popular from 1983-1986?

Answer: In 1983-1986, Cabbage Patch Kids were so popular that Cabbage Patch riots occurred as parents literally fought to obtain the dolls.

80's

④ What year did the Berlin Wall fall?

Answer: The Berlin Wall fell in 1989.

80's

⑤ How many Americans watched the O.J. Simpson trial verdict on live television?

- A. 11 million people
- B. 47 million people
- C. 95 million people
- D. 150 million people

Answer: During the OJ Simpson case on October 3, 1995, 57% of Americans were watching when O.J. Simpson was declared "not guilty." This was.....

D. 150 million people

This was so large that phone companies noted a 60% drop in usage during the trial.

⑥ What year did the World Wide Web go public?

Answer: 4 years after the proposal for "an idea of linked information systems," the World Wide Web was made accessible to the public on April 30, 1993.

ROUND 15.2
QUESTIONS FOR PARENTS

(7) Who was the best-selling artist of the 2000s?

Answer: It was Eminem who sold 32.25 million albums in the 2000s, and the Beatles were just behind him, selling 32 million albums in the 2000s decade.

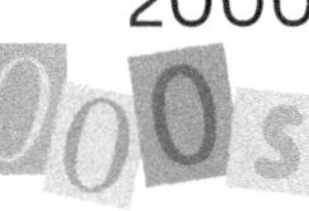

(8) What year was the first iPhone released?

Answer: After introducing the iPhone in January of 2007, Steve Jobs launched the iPhone just 6 months later on June 29, 2007. The 4G model was priced at $499, and the 8G model was priced at $599. Critics said it was way too expensive to ever succeed in the market.

(9) What was the top travel destination in the 2010s?

Answer: The most popular tourist destination of the 2010s was France, which had around 77 million visitors per year. Coming in second was Spain, with about 72 million visitors per year, followed by the United States, with 70 million visitors per year.

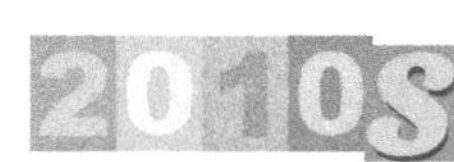

(10) What category 4 hurricane hit the U.S. Gulf Coast in 2017?

Answer: It was Hurricane Harvey which caused extensive damage and flooding, particularly in Houston, Texas.

Round 16

Cars

Welcome to Round 16!

This round will be another standard round.

There will be 9 questions, with questions 8 and 9 being worth 2 points.

The category for this round is cars!

Let's get right into it!

Kids

 Points

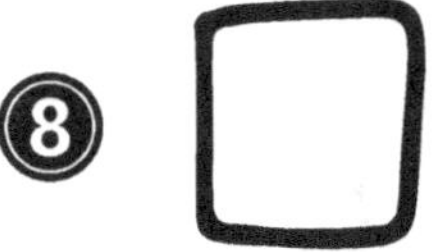

 Points

Total Points =

Parents

 Points

Total Points =

ROUND 16.1
QUESTIONS FOR KIDS

1 What is the most popular car color?

- **A.** Silver
- **B.** White
- **C.** Blue
- **D.** Black

Answer: The most popular car color is

- **B.** White

About 25 % of all cars driven are white.

2 How long is the average Formula 1 pit stop?

- **A.** 2.5 seconds
- **B.** 5 seconds
- **C.** 9 seconds
- **D.** 12 seconds

Answer: The average Formula 1 pitstop only takes about

- **A.** 2.5 Seconds

The fastest pitstop time ever recorded was 1.82 seconds.

3 What year was the first car invented?

- **A.** 1796
- **B.** 1834
- **C.** 1886
- **D.** 1907

Answer: The first car was invented in

- **C.** 1886

Karl Benz submitted a patent application on January 29, 1886, for his gas-powered vehicle. The patent number 37,435 is considered as the car's birth certificate.

ROUND 16.1
QUESTIONS FOR KIDS

(4) What do you call a car that's lost its wheels and its muffler?

Answer: You call it exhausted.

(5) What do you call a car that is popular with the ladies?

Answer: A pickup truck.

(6) Who was the man that reduced the cost of producing cars by implementing an assembly line for making cars?

Answer: In 1913, Henry Ford and his employees successfully began using the assembly line to make cars.

(7) Which car brand makes the Mustang?

Answer: It is a Ford Mustang after all.

(8) What country consumes the most gas every year?

Answer: The United States is the largest gas consumer, using around 22% of the world's yearly consumed gas.

(9) What does SUV stand for?

Answer: It stands for Sport Utility Vehicle.

Random Fun Fact?

The highest mileage ever recorded on a car was 2,850,000 miles, which is equal to driving around the Earth about 100 times.

ROUND 16.2
QUESTIONS FOR PARENTS

① Where is the "World's Largest Truck Stop" located?

- **A.** Texas
- **B.** California
- **C.** Georgia
- **D.** Iowa

Answer: The world's largest truck stop is in

- **D.** Iowa

This truck stop is the Iowa 80 stop, located about 1 mile north of a small town named Walcott. It has eight restaurants and a chiropractor.

② As of today, who are the 2 largest car manufacturers in the world?

- **A.** Ford and Toyota
- **B.** Tesla and Honda
- **C.** General Motors and Honda
- **D.** Volkswagon AG and Toyota

The two largest car manufacturers are

- **D.** Volkswagon AG and Toyota

Volkswagen AG, based out of Germany, is the largest manufacturer, and Toyota, based out of Japan, is the second largest.

③ On August 5th 1914 the world's first electric traffic signal was put into place on the corner of Euclid Avenue and East 105th Street in....

- **A.** New York City
- **B.** Boston
- **C.** Chicago
- **D.** Cleveland

Answer: On August 5th 1914 the first electric traffic signal was put into place on the corner of Euclid Avenue and East 105th Street in

- **D.** Cleveland Ohio

ROUND 16.2
QUESTIONS FOR PARENTS

④ Why do softball players go to the dealership?

Answer: They want a sales pitch.

⑤ What is a sheep's favorite car?

Answer: It is a Laaamb-orghini.

⑥ What does the term automobile stand for?

Answer: Auto (is the prefix for self) and mobile (is the prefix for moving). So, automobile stands for self-moving.

⑦ What country are Lamborghini's made in?

Answer: Since Lamborghini's founding in 1963, Lamborghinis have been produced in Sant'Agata Bolognese, which is a small town in Italy home to around 8,000 people.

⑧ What animal is on the Porsche logo?

Answer: It is a horse.

⑨ What country was the airbag invented in?

Answer: The airbag was actually invented by more than 1 person. Both American John W. Hetrick and German Walter Linderer filed separate and independent airbag patents around the same time in the early 1950s. So, if you said America or Germany, you are correct!

Round 17

Family

Welcome to round 17!

This round is going to be a little bit different. The way this round works is that..

Each team will answer questions about the other team, so

the parents will answer questions about the kids.

And before the question is asked, the kids will pick a representative from their team.

The representative chosen is whom the question is being asked about.

Then, the question will be asked about the representative, and the parents must answer before the music runs out.

And vice versa for when the kids answer questions about the parents.

This might sound confusing, but let's practice with 2 examples.

Let's say that the kids are answering questions about the parents.

Question 1 (*Team parents select a representative from team parents and make sure team kids know who the representative is.*)

You should have the representative selected by now.

What is the birthday of the representative team parents have chosen? Team kids answer the question.

Let's practice another example .

Now, the parents are answering questions about the kids.

Question 2: *Team kids select your representative and make sure team parents know who the representative is.*

What is the representative's favorite color? Now, team parents answer the question.

So I hope you understand how this round works; this is a really fun spin-off of regular trivia.

There will be 10 questions, each worth 1 point.

The kids will start off by answering 10 questions in a row. Then, the parents will answer 10 in a row. We hope you enjoy the round.

Kids

Total Points = __________

Parents

Total Points = __________

101

ROUND 17.1
QUESTIONS FOR KIDS

1 Team parents, select your representative. **What was the representative's first-ever job?**

2 Team parents, select your representative. **What genre of music did the representative enjoy when they were younger? (think ages 16-25)**

3 Team parents, select your representative. **What is the representative's all-time favorite vacation spot?**

4 Team parents, select your representative. **What is the representative's favorite season of the year?**

5 Team parents, select your representative. **If the parent's representative could live anywhere in the world, where would it be?**

6 Team parents, select your representative. **What is the parent's representative's favorite book?**

7 Team parents, select your representative. **What was the last movie the parent's representative went to?**

8 Team parents, select your representative. **Would the parent's representative rather win the lottery or live twice as long?**

9 Team parents, select your representative. **Would the parent's representative rather know every language in the world or speak with animals?**

10 Team parents, select your representative. **Would the parent's representative rather lose their vision or their ability to heal?**

ROUND 17.2
QUESTIONS FOR PARENTS

① Team parents, select your representative. **What is the scariest thing the kid's representative has ever done?**

② Team kids, select your representative. **If the kid's representative were to describe themselves with 1 word, what would it be?**

③ Team kids, select your representative. **What is the best gift that the kid's representative has ever received?**

④ Team kids, select your representative. **What is the kid's representative's favorite food?**

⑤ Team kids, select your representative. **How many pillows does the kid's representative sleep with?**

⑥ Team kids, select your representative. **How long of showers does the kid's representative take?**

⑦ Team kids, select your representative. **What is the kid's representative's favorite subject in school?**

⑧ Team kids, select your representative. **Would the kid's representative rather make a phone call or send a text?**

⑨ Team kids, select your representative. **Would the kid's representative rather explore space or the ocean?**

⑩ Team kids, select your representative. **Would the kid's representative rather be too hot or too cold?**

Round 18

Sports

Welcome to round 18!

This will be another regular round, by now you should know the drill.

There are 9 questions, with questions 8 and 9 being worth 2 points.

The category for this round is sports.

Let's get into it!

Kids

 Points

 Points

Total Points = __________

Parents

 Points

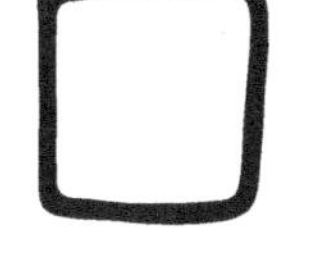

 Points

Total Points = __________

ROUND 18.1
QUESTIONS FOR KIDS

1 Who is the only NBA player in history to win Most Valuable Player, Coach, and Executive of the year?

A. Michael Jordan

B. Larry Bird

C. Phil Jackson

D. Lebron James

Answer: It was

B. Larry Bird

Larry Bird spent his entire career as a player with the Boston Celtics, where he won 3 NBA titles. From 1997 to 2000, he was the Indiana Pacers' head coach, then in 2003, he became the team's president of basketball operations.

2 What country won the first World Cup?

A. Uruguay

B. Brazil

C. Germany

D. Argentina

Answer: On July 30, 1930, in the first World Cup final, Argentina was defeated by

A. Uruguay

Uruguay won 4-2, making Uruguay a small South American country between Brazil and Argentina, the first-ever World Cup champions.

ROUND 18.1
QUESTIONS FOR KIDS

③ What is the most amount of red cards given in a single soccer game?

A. 12

B. 21

C. 36

Answer: In 2011, referee Damien Rubino gave out

C. 36 red cards

④ What sport do insects like to play?

Answer: They play cricket.

⑤ Why did the football team go to the bank?

Answer: To get a quarter back.

⑥ Who is the most decorated Olympian? Meaning which Olympian has won the most Olympic medals?

Answer: American swimmer Michael Phelps is the most decorated Olympian winning 28 Olympic medals, with 23 of them being gold and 13 of the 23 gold medals being individual events.

⑦ What sport causes the most injuries in the United States every year?

Answer: Believe it or not, basketball actually has more injuries than any other sport, followed by football, soccer, and baseball.

⑧ What is the national sport of Canada?

Answer: The national sport of Canada is lacrosse.

⑨ In what country did the first ancient Olympic games take place?

Answer: In the summer of 776 B.C. the first ever Olympics were held at Olympia, a place in Greece where people would worship their gods. The Olympics were actually created to honor the greek god Zues.

1 What is the highest score that a PGA player has made on a par-4?

A. 8 strokes

B. 10 strokes

C. 16 strokes

D. 21 strokes

Answer: On April 14, 2011, at the ninth hole of the Valero Texas Open. Kevin Na played the worst ever par-4 hole on the PGA Tour since the tour began, recording a

C. 16

2 Which of the following NFL head coaches has the highest winning percentage in the postseason?

A. Bill Belichick

B. Jimmy Johnson

C. Mike Tomlin

D. Barry Switzer

Answer: It is

D. Barry Switzer

Barry Switzer, who was 5-2 in the playoffs, has the best percentage, winning 71.4% of his playoff games.

3 How many members of the Spanish basketball team from the 2000 Summer Paralympics were eventually determined not to have a disability?

A. 4 players

B. 6 players

C. 10 players

Answer: There were

C. 10 players

When it was discovered that 10 of the 12 participants were not disabled, Spain lost its gold medal.

④ When do tennis players wake up?

Answer: They wake up at ten-ish.

⑤ What animal is the best at baseball?

Answer: A bat.

⑥ What was the first televised sport in the United States?

Answer: Baseball was the first sport to ever be broadcasted on American television. Princeton and Columbia played the historic match on May 17, 1939.

⑦ What is it called when a bowler makes 3 consecutive strikes?

Answer: It is called a turkey.

⑧ What do the letters BMX stand for?

Answer: BMX Stands for Bicycle Motocross.

⑨ What was the Marathon named after?

Answer: The name Marathon comes from a Greek messenger named Pheidippides. He was a messenger sent from the battlefield of Marathon to Athens to announce that the Persian army had lost the Battle of Marathon. Pheidippides is believed to have ran 26.2 miles without stopping, and when he got to Athens, he exclaimed, "We have won!" before he died from exhaustion.

Round 19

History

Welcome to round 19!

This will be another regular round, by now you should know the drill.

There are 9 questions, with questions 8 and 9 being worth 2 points.

The category for this round is history.

Let's get into it!

Kids

Points

Points

Total Points = _______________

Parents

Points

Points

Total Points = _______________

ROUND 19.1
QUESTIONS FOR KIDS

1 Which city became the first to ever reach a population of 1 million people?

> A. Beijing

> B. London

> C. Rome

> D. Alexandria

Answer: The first city to reach a population of 1 million was

> C. Rome

2 Who is known for having a large signature on the U.S. Declaration of Independence?

> A. William Whipple

> B. Benjamin Franklin

> C. John Hancock

> D. George Washington

Answer: It was

> C. John Hancock

3 When the Mayflower set sail for the New World in 1620, how many people were on board?

> A. 58 people

> B. 102 people

> C. 208 people

Answer: The Mayflower had

> B. 102 people

There were 102 passengers on the Mayflower, and it is assumed that of the 102, the crew made up roughly 30 of them. There were only 53 survivors after the first winter.

ROUND 19.1
QUESTIONS FOR KIDS

④ I'll always be in the past, but I am being created 24/7. The future has no effect on me. What am I?

Answer: I am History.

⑤ Who made King Arthur's round table?

Answer: Sir Cumference did.

⑥ What year did King Ferdinand and Queen Isabella of Spain fund Christopher Columbus's voyage to find a better trade route and explore the unknown?

Answer: Christopher Columbus's voyage was funded and began in 1492.

⑦ Who was president during the Cuban Missile Crisis?

Answer: The president was John F. Kennedy.

⑧ What were the first pillows made out of?

Answer: In 7,000 BC, the first ever pillows were made of stone, and the oldest known pillow dates back to Mesopotamia over 9,000 years ago.

⑨ Who was the first Catholic Pope?

Answer: St. Peter was the first pope of the Catholic Church, and he was also known as one of Jesus's original 12 disciples.

Random Fun Fact?

Abraham Lincoln is in the Wrestling Hall of Fame. With close to 300 contests and only 1 loss, he was officially inducted into the National Wrestling Hall of Fame as an "Outstanding American."

ROUND 19.2
QUESTIONS FOR PARENTS

1 Who was the first U.S. president to be impeached?

- **A.** Richard Nixon
- **B.** Herbert Hoover
- **C.** Andrew Johnson
- **D.** William Howard Taft

Answer: On February 24, 1868 the first president to get impeached was

C. Andrew Johnson

Following Abraham Lincoln's assassination, Andrew Johnson was appointed president. However, shortly after, he was impeached due to congress believing he went too far in pleasing the South and failing to defend the rights of those who had been set free from slavery.

2 Who served as the United Kingdom's first prime minister?

- **A.** George Greenville
- **B.** Robert Walpole
- **C.** Henry Pelham
- **D.** Winston Churchill

Answer: The first prime minister was

B. Robert Walpole

Despite the fact that Prime Minister was not the official title during his time. Walpole served the role of Prime Minister for the longest period in British history—from 1721 to 1742.

ROUND 19.2
QUESTIONS FOR PARENTS

3 In 1952, which German man was given the opportunity to serve as Israel's second president?

A. Albert Einstein

B. Leo von Klenze

C. Albert Speer

D. Wilfred Martens

Answer: Israel offered the role to

A. Albert Einstein

In 1952, Albert Einstein, a Jew but not an Israeli citizen, was given the chance to become president but declined.

4 What fruit is always a part of history?

Answer: A date.

5 Where do kings, queens, knights and bishops go to war?

Answer: They all go to war in chess.

6 What global organization was founded in 1945, right after World War II?

Answer: After World War II, the United Nations was created in an effort to avoid future wars.

7 What is the name of the first Soviet satellite launched into space in 1957?

Answer: The first Soviet satellite launched into space was called the Sputnik 1. It was launched on October 4, 1957, and sent a radio signal back to Earth for 3 weeks until its battery ran out.

8 Which war was started because a pig was shot?

Answer: It was the Pig War, which was a conflict between the U.S. and Great Britain over the San Juan Islands. Fortunately, the pig was the only casualty of the war.

9 Who is generally considered the "father of history"?

Answer: It is Herodotus.

Round 20

Repeat Questions

Welcome to round 20!

This is the final round, and I hope you have been paying attention to the previous rounds because all the questions in this round will come from previous chapters.

There will be 1 question asked from each of the previous rounds.

Every question in this round is worth 1 point, Good luck!

Kids

1
2
3
4
5
6
7
8
9
10
11
12
13
14
15
16
17

Total Points = ______________

Parents

1
2
3
4
5
6
7
8
9
10
11
12
13
14
15
16
17

Total Points = ______________

117

ROUND 20.1
QUESTIONS FOR KIDS

① Where was the Caesar Salad invented?

Answer: It was invented in Mexico.

② What does the word booyah mean?

Answer: The word booyah is used to express joy, happiness, or being elated.

③ Which river flows through London?

Answer: The River flowing through London is River Thames.

④ What is the fastest-flying bird in the world?

Answer: The fastest flying bird is a Peregrine Falcon.

⑤ According to tradition, what time should April Fools' Day jokes stop?

Answer: An April Fools' joke should stop at 12 PM.

⑥ What can go up and down without physically moving?

Answer: It is the temperature.

⑦ What was the name of the spacecraft that carried the first-ever astronauts into space?

Answer: It was Apollo 11.

⑧ Name the movie that this iconic quote comes from: *"You're gonna need a bigger boat."*

Answer: This quote comes from Jaws.

⑨ What was the theme song for the 1982 film, Rocky III?

Answer: It was the "Eye of the Tiger."

⑩ How many kids does Angelina Jolie have?

Answer: Angelina Jolie has 6 kids.

ROUND 20.1
QUESTIONS FOR KIDS

11 I am very light, yet no one can throw me far. What am I?

Answer: I am a feather.

12 Which Indian catholic nun said, "Spread love wherever you go. Let no one ever come to you without leaving happier."

Answer: It was Mother Teresa.

13 What war did the United States get involved in that lasted from June 25, 1950, to July 27, 1953?

Answer: It was the Korean War.

14 What was the popular 70's hairstyle that involved mid-length to long hair, brushed back and outward at the sides?

Answer: It was the feathered look.

15 Why did the car break up with his girlfriend?

Answer: She kept taking him for granite.

16 What do the letters BMX stand for?

Answer: BMX Stands for Bicycle Motocross.

17 Who is considered the "father of history"?

Answer: The father of history is considered to be Herodotus.

Random Fun Fact?

More than 50% of the people in the world have never made or received a phone call.

ROUND 20.2
ANSWERS FOR PARENTS

1 Which U.S. state is the biggest producer of coffee?

Answer: It is Hawaii.

2 What does bussin mean?

Answer: The term bussin means delicious.

3 Which one of the following countries is further north? Scotland or Netherlands?

Answer: Scotland is further north.

4 How many times can a hummingbird flap its wings per second?

Answer: A hummingbird can flap its wings 80 times per second.

5 How many national holidays are there in America?

Answer: There are 11 nationally recognized holidays in America.

6 What is the hard outer covering on insects called?

Answer: The hard outer covering is called an exoskeleton.

7 How many planets in our Solar System are surrounded by rings?

Answer: There are 4 planets with rings. Saturn, Neptune, Uranus and Jupiter.

8 Who plays Adonis Creed in the Creed series?

Answer: This actor is Michael B. Jordan.

9 Who wrote the song "We Don't Talk Anymore"?

Answer: "We Don't Talk Anymore" was written by Charlie Puth.

10 Where did Prince William meet Kate Middleton?

Answer: The pair first met at the University of St. Andrews.

ROUND 20.2
ANSWERS FOR PARENTS

11 Even though I'm lighter than a feather, no one can hold me for 7 minutes. What am I?

Answer: I am your breath.

12 Which Founding Father said "Well done is better than well said."

Answer: It was Benjamin Franklin.

13 What state is the Tomb of the Unknown Soldier located in?

Answer: The Tomb of the Unknown Soldier is located in Virginia.

14 What was the name of the first-ever cloned sheep?

Answer: Its name was Dolly.

15 What do you call a car that is good with the ladies?

Answer: A pickup truck.

16 What is the record number of red cards given in a single soccer game?

Answer: It is 36 red cards.

17 How many passengers were aboard the Mayflower when it set sail for the New World in 1620?

Answer: There were 102 passengers.

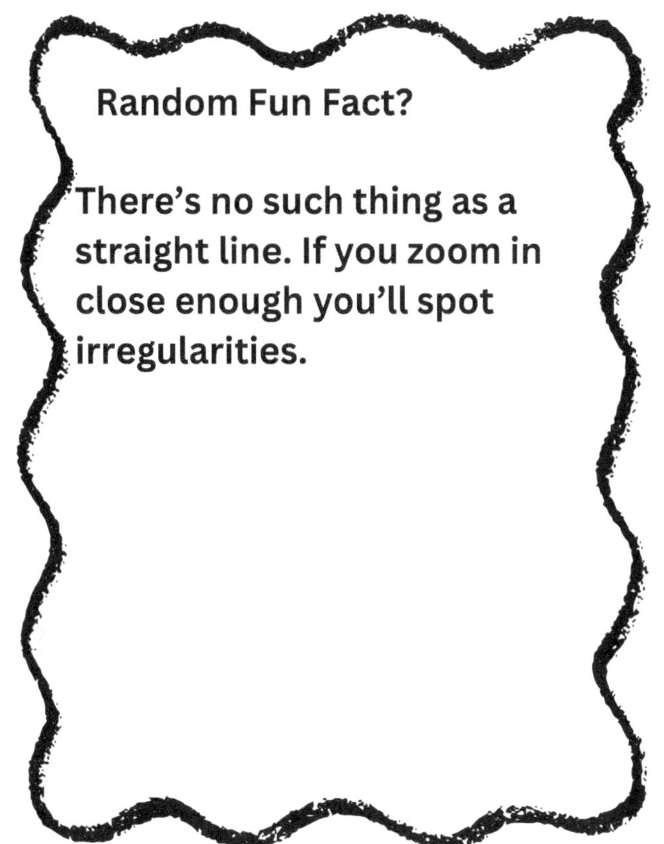

Random Fun Fact?

There's no such thing as a straight line. If you zoom in close enough you'll spot irregularities.

FINAL SCORE
FINAL SCORE

_______________   _______________

KIDS   PARENTS

Family Game Night

If you have 30 seconds we would apreciate a reivew!

REFUND
POLICY

If you were unsatisfied with the book send us an email and we will refund you no questions asked.

In the email please describe why you did not like the book and how we can improve it. We honor our word and will fully reimburse unsatisfied customers.

If you would like a refund please email our customer support team member

willwarren111@gmail.com

- ☑ Paypal
- ☑ Zel
- ☑ Wise
- ☑ Payoneer